500 of the
WORLD'S BEST
Web Sites

Series Editor: Colleen Collier
Revised Series Editor: Lucy Dear
Research: Jodie Geddes, Colleen Collier
Additional Contributors: Jane Purcell, Linley Clode, Tonia Serov, Christine Poutney, Richard Skinner, Sue Curran, Ann Marangos, Sarah Wells
Page Design and Layout: Linley Clode
Cover Design: Sol Communications Ltd

Published by:
Lagoon Books
PO Box 311, KT2 5QW, UK
PO Box 990676, Boston, MA 02199, USA

www.lagoongames.com

ISBN: 1-902813-30-8

Printed in Singapore.

500 of the
WORLD'S BEST
Web Sites
LAGOON
BOOKS

Whilst every care has been taken to ensure the material in this book is accurate at the time of press, the constantly changing nature of the Internet makes it impossible to guarantee that every address will be correct or every web site available.

Every effort will be made to revise and update sites on our web site.

Lagoon will assume neither liability nor responsibility to any person or entity with respect to any loss, damage or suitability of the web sites contained in this book.

CONTENTS

INTRODUCTION

'The Internet is a tidal wave...drowning those who don't learn to swim in its waves' – Bill Gates

Over the past few years, many guides to the Internet have been written explaining how to access the Net and how to use it. But now everyone's looking for a fun and easy-to-use guide to the best sites, so here it is!

This stunning 288-page directory lists 500 of the World's Best Web Sites, and is subdivided into eight amazing chapters, according to subject, to make searching even easier!

The research has been carried out by an avid team of fun-loving Internet surfers, whose brief was to find the best sites on the web for you to enjoy – which is just what they did! Go to p58 or p99 to see what I mean!

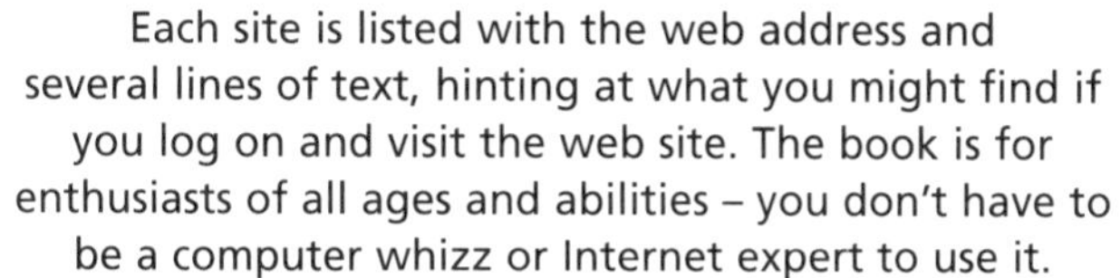

Each site is listed with the web address and several lines of text, hinting at what you might find if you log on and visit the web site. The book is for enthusiasts of all ages and abilities – you don't have to be a computer whizz or Internet expert to use it.

Amongst the 500 fantastic web sites listed here, you will be able to find out...

...How to see the world for only $25 a day
...Where to get hold of theater tickets six months before they go on sale
...Where buried treasure is waiting to be discovered
...How to create the home and garden of your dreams
...Where to obtain free detailed maps of all the cities in the world
...What your chances of alien abduction are
...How to download new and classic films to watch on your computer

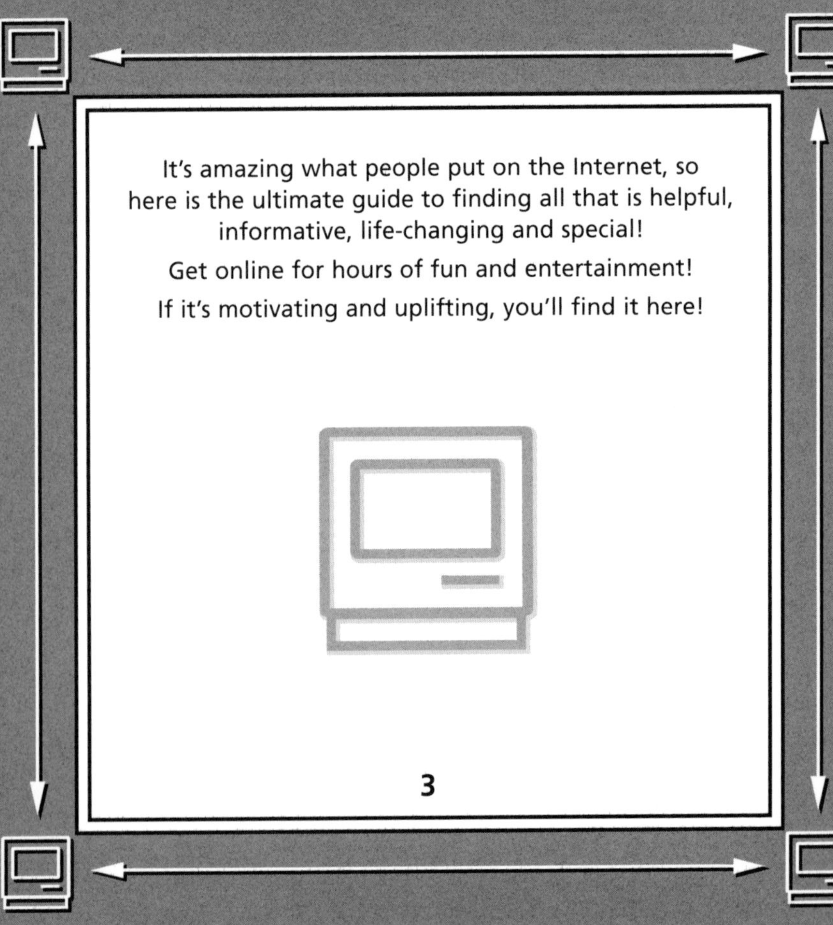

It's amazing what people put on the Internet, so here is the ultimate guide to finding all that is helpful, informative, life-changing and special!

Get online for hours of fun and entertainment!

If it's motivating and uplifting, you'll find it here!

1

Entertainment

The Simpsons

http://www.thesimpsons.com/

This is the official Simpsons' site and is the one with the best facts! Check out the biographies of the characters and the actors who play them.

Who Killed Kenny?

http://www.comedycentral.com/southpark

'South Park' has taken over from where 'The Simpsons' left off. Buy merchandise at this site and why not join the South Park Booster Club?

Fox

http://www.foxmovies.com

Check out this site for all the latest trailers, news and reviews straight from Hollywood.

International Movie Database

http://www.imdb.com

You can search here for almost any film ever made (it contains over 170,000 listings!). The reviews are upbeat and you can submit your own too.

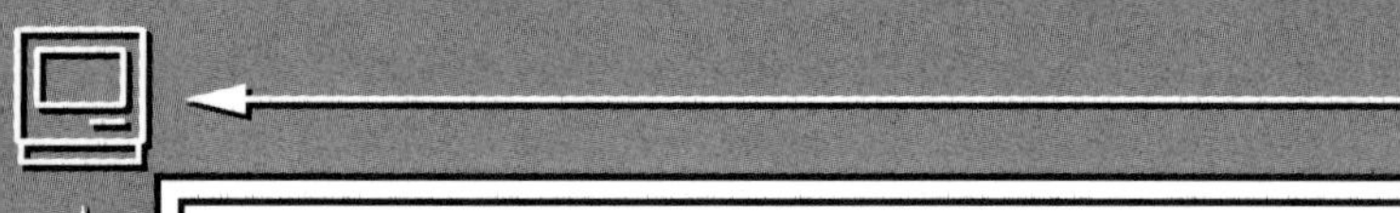

Film.com

http://www.film.com

This is a film site that has a huge range of reviews, quizzes and polls you can get involved in, plus interviews with top directors and actors.

Film Four

http://www.filmfour.com

Film Four are alternative filmmakers, constantly producing films that are both original and controversial such as the hit 'Trainspotting'. Click on the links to find out about their next production.

Hollywood

http://www.hollywood.com

This glitzy, jam-packed site will give you the latest on all the upcoming movies straight from the heart of Tinsel Town.

Wonderful World of Disney

http://www.disney.com

Disney is still churning out some of the greatest movies for kids. Log on for a trip down memory lane and see some of your cartoon favorites.

Film Unlimited

http://film.guardian.co.uk/

This site has some of the best reviewers working for them – so you end up with a great mixture of tastes and can choose a film best suited to you.

Subtitles

http://www.mrqe.com

When you are looking for an original foreign film that can't be found at your local video store, look here for the best selection.

Brady Encyclopedia

http://davidbrady.com/eb/

Welcome to the swinging site of the family who were so squeaky clean that germs would have trouble surviving in the same room! Delve into an archive of Brady gossip and find out what the stars are doing now.

Kick the Bucket!

http://www.dpsinfo.com/dps.html

Is that actor really dead? Or was it just his performance? Check here to find out if your favorite star has gone to the Chateau Marmont in the sky.

Industry Gossip!

http://www.cinescape.com

This fab site will give you an escape from the daily grind by keeping you bang up-to-date with all the film industry news and gossip.

Miramax

http://www.miramax.com

Miramax has produced some great films of late. Use their site to take a look at what people are currently watching around the world.

Jerry Springer Online

http://www.universalstudios.com/tv/jerryspringer/

Cussing, shouting and a deluge of domestic drama – it's just a regular show for Springer fans! Get all the dirt here.

Xena, Warrior Princess

http://www.xenafan.com

Fans of the leather-clad, high-kicking princess will love this Xena bonanza – get the low-down on the stars and chat to other Lucy Lawless worshippers.

Euro Cinema

http://www.eurocinema.com

For a small price, you can download and watch any number of new and old European films. Très bon!

Planet Trekkie

http://www.startrek.com

You will be spaced out when you clap your eyes and pointy ears onto this well-designed site. Go on a tour of 'The Enterprise' at warp factor nine!

Alternative Entertainment

http://www.aentv.com

Watch classic films and TV programs at this alternative entertainment network – they also have a very good section on how the films were styled and made.

Get Into Movies

http://www.paramount.com/studio/homecareer_frame.html

If you are desperate to get into the world of movies, there are lots of jobs listed on this studio job site.

Blunt Review

http://www.bluntreview.com

Emily Blunt is one opinionated movie critic, so her reviews are funny and straight to the point! Check out her no-nonsense views before choosing a film.

Great Dames for Sale!

http://www.geocities.com/CapeCanaveral/5958/funnews.html

Fun page of bloopers, misprints and poorly worded phrases recently published in newspapers that will have you chuckling all the way to the news-stand.

People

http://www.people.com

The US gossip and celebrity magazine is now online! Find out who is dating who and what diet they are on!

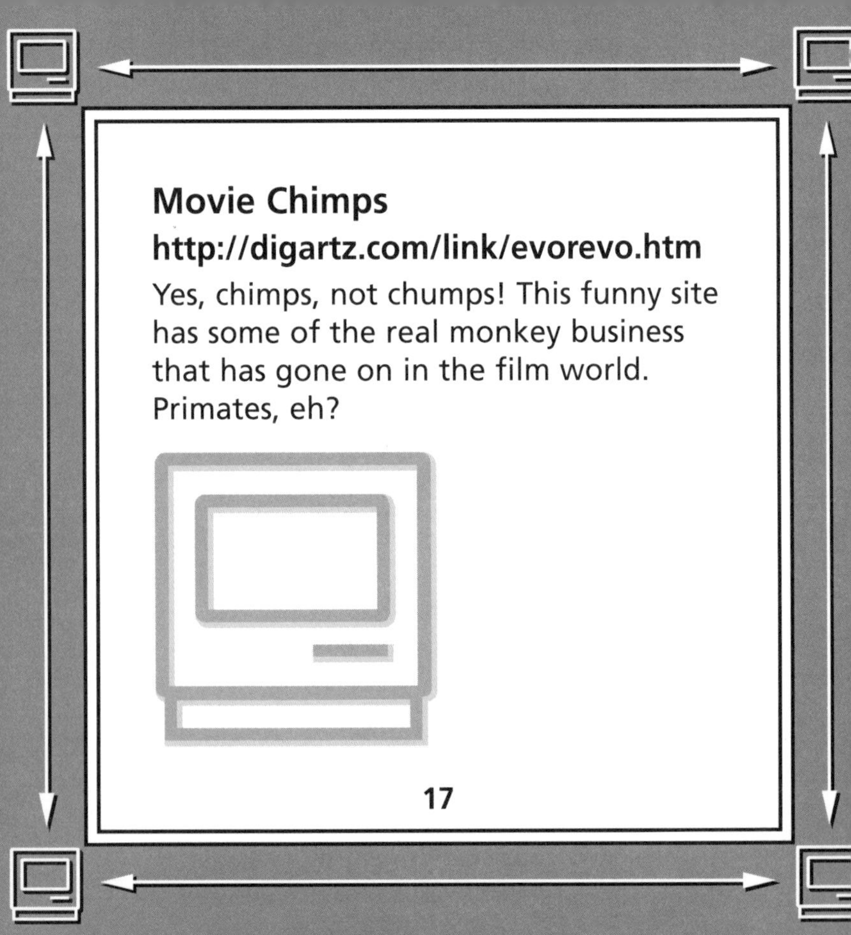

Movie Chimps

http://digartz.com/link/evorevo.htm

Yes, chimps, not chumps! This funny site has some of the real monkey business that has gone on in the film world. Primates, eh?

Hollywood Reporter

http://www.hollywoodreporter.com

This is a kind of Louella Parsons online detailing all the latest star news, gossip and trivia.

Sam and Dean

http://www.rinkworks.com/movies

It's always better to get more than one opinion on a film – so Sam and Dean have combined their love of movies and compiled a list of bite-sized reviews.

Script-o-rama

http://www.script-o-rama.com

Calling all scriptwriting wannabes! Log onto this site to take a look at the original scripts from hundreds of movies such as 'Alien' and 'The Doors'.

Low Budget Bonanza

http://www.filmscouts.com

Quite often, you will find some absolute gems in the short-film world. It's well worth checking this site out to see the Stanley Kubricks of tomorrow.

Magic Land

http://www.magicland.org

The place to come if you are a fledgling magician or an old hand, full of tricks, chat and bios for you to enjoy.

Media Nugget

http://www.medianugget.com/archive/20001019.html

Impress your friends! Visit this daily-updated site that provides bite-sized music, art and film reviews to keep you firmly in the know.

Long Live Theater!

http://www.theatredb.com

A jam-packed, searchable archive of theater, past, present and future, to fully entertain theater buffs everywhere.

Movie Tunes

http://www.movietunes.com

This tuneful site is dedicated to the unsung heroes of the movie world – namely the composers! It's these guys that make your heart swell when the screen lovers finally kiss.

Stomp Tokyo

http://www.stomptokyo.com/

This excellent site takes you back to all the film greats such as 'Godzilla' and 'Fungus of Terror' and gives them a lava lamp rating!

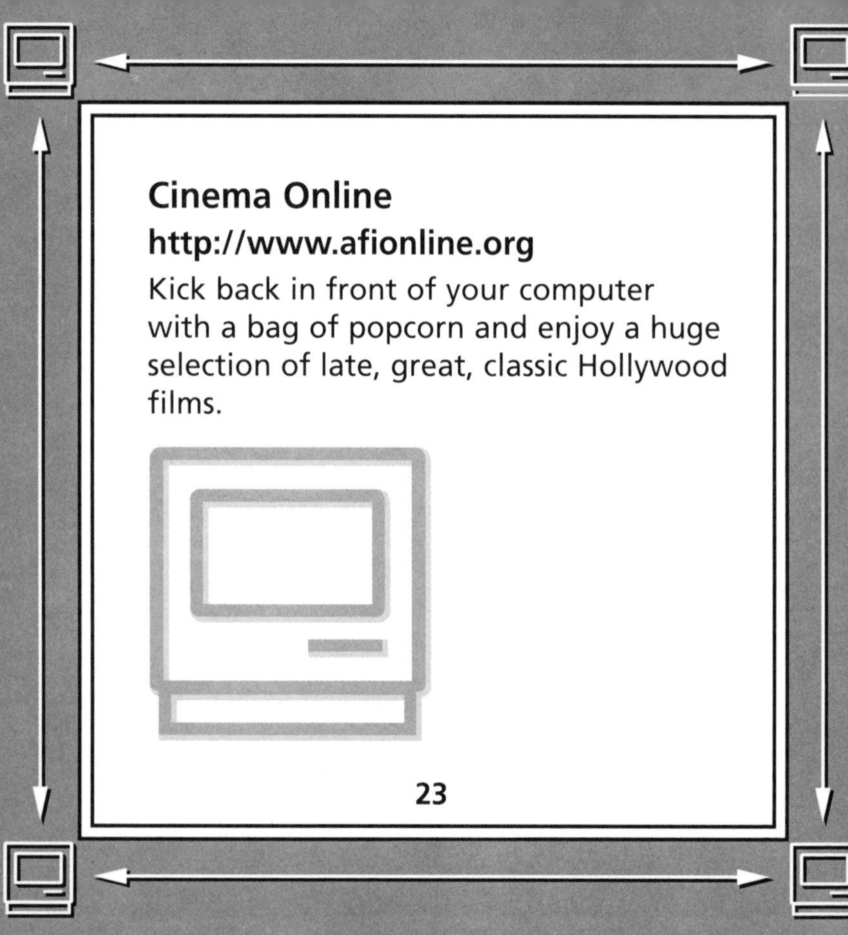

Cinema Online

http://www.afionline.org

Kick back in front of your computer with a bag of popcorn and enjoy a huge selection of late, great, classic Hollywood films.

Pseudo

http://www.pseudo.com

A TV channel especially set up for the Net – watch all your favorite TV programs and sitcoms from your own computer!

Film 100

http://www.film100.com

Who are the most influential people in the film industry? Find out the top 100 directors, producers and, of course, actors here at this site.

The Show Must Go On!

http://www.geocities.com/Broadway/8244

Share your own theatrical calamities and read about hellish shows where it has all gone horribly wrong! It's not always all right on the night!

Movie List

http://www.movie-list.com

Download 15-second previews of all the upcoming films to hit the silver screen. Be warned though, the download takes quite a long time so be patient!

Heard That Before?

http://www.moviecliches.com

Did you know that the most worn-out phrase in the movies is 'Let's get outta here!' Check out this smorgasbord of movie clichés – you will split your sides!

Soap Sensaton

http://members.aol.com/soaplinks

Are you a soap addict? Then visit this site which links you to all the hot news about your favorites.

Oo-eer Matron!

http://www.carryonline.com

If you are a fan of the British institution that is 'Carry On' films, then you will love this site, which is full of good ol' British humor.

Free Broadcast

http://www.broadcast.com

Look and listen, for this site has a free download of all the current TV and radio programs. Tune in and watch the world!

Cannes Do!

http://www.festival-cannes.fr

If the glitter and glamor of the Cannes film festival is your scene, then you'll want to step out in style and log onto this site full of past and present images and events.

Musical Reviews

http://www.dailyvault.com

Newly released albums are reviewed daily at this mega music site, so you can find out what's hot and what's not before everyone else.

Bad Blood

http://www.ohthehumanity.com

This site spares you the chore of sifting through all of the bad movies in the horror genre and gives a run-down of some of the worst shockers in film history.

Roast Turkeys

http://www.badmovies.org

A must for all bad-movie fans with plenty to choose from. Check out the story behind 'Cannibal Women in the Avocado Jungle of Death'! No, I haven't heard of it either!

Jurassic Punk

http://www.jurassicpunk.com

This site has nothing to do with a dinosaur park but is a monster site featuring regularly updated trailers of the up-and-coming blockbusters.

Turn It Off!

http://www.thestinkers.com

Here's your chance to vote for those billion-dollar films that stank out the screen like a six-week old burger! Sharpen your knives and get stuck in.

Theater Direct

http://www.broadwayonline.com

If you're planning a trip to London or New York and want to pre-book theater tickets to the hottest shows, then do so here!

What's on Stage?

http://www.whatsonstage.com

Search for UK theater and musical tickets here for up to six months before they go on sale and check out the fantastic review section.

Time Out

http://www.timeout.com

If it's entertainment you're after, then *Time Out* will have the answers – this online guide features the hottest up-to-date listings in over 30 happening cities.

Comedy Butchers

http://www.comedybutchers.com

These guys have their own unique brand of comedy and showcase it via the Net. Saves the humiliation of being booed off stage, I guess!

Comedy Central

http://www.comedycentral.com

Parent site devoted to US comedies – everything you need to know and downloads that will make you laugh out loud!

Book Browse

http://www.bookbrowse.com

A literary smorgasbord of current books, reviewed and excerpted for your reading pleasure.

Radio Days

http://www.midnightscience.com

A site dedicated to helping you build crystal radio sets – full of tips on how to do it and where to get advice.

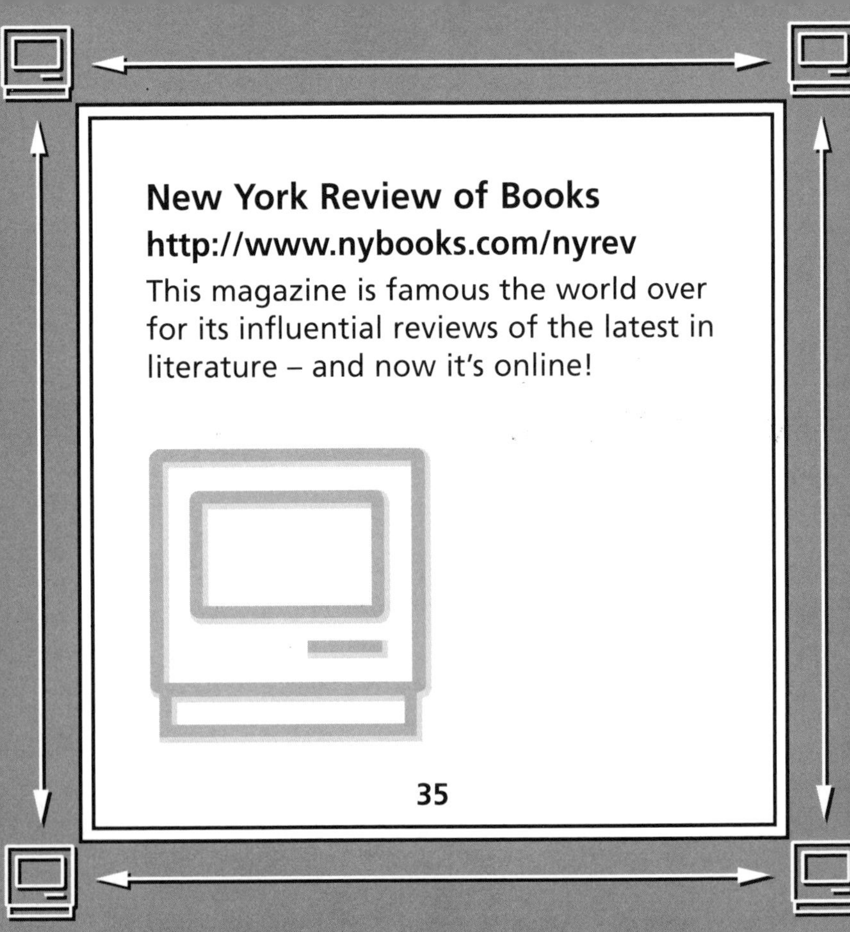

New York Review of Books

http://www.nybooks.com/nyrev

This magazine is famous the world over for its influential reviews of the latest in literature – and now it's online!

Book Fanatic

http://www.bookwire.com

This detailed site gives you a first-hand look at the book business and is full of industry news, literary events and author interviews.

Gonna Write a Classic

http://www.musdoc.com/classical

Everything you could want to know about the world of classical music, from composers to record labels.

Play It Again!

http://www.sheetmusicdirect.com

This musical site contains the largest selection of copyrighted sheet music solely for your playing pleasure – purchase it online and it will be delivered in seconds to your own printer!

Live Onstage Tonight

http://www.liveconcerts.com

Soak up that unbeatable atmosphere by logging on to this site where you can download live performances from top artists online.

Movie-a-minute

http://rinkworks.com/movieaminute

Too many movies to see and not enough time? Click on here to find the funny ultra-condensed versions of the big hits!

Daily Poetry

http://www.poems.com

Pause for thought and take a break by reading the contemporary poem that appears daily at this literary site.

Entertainment Express

http://www.mvc.infront.co.uk/

A one-stop shop full of CDs, videos, DVDs and games – full of great discounts and charts to make your choice even easier.

Virtual Festivals

http://www.virtual-festivals.com

From Woodstock to Glastonbury, here you will find the latest line-ups, booking details and news of the best of the year's hot events.

2

Weird and Wacky

The Bureau of Missing Socks

http://www.funbureau.com/

Find out more about one of the world's most frustrating mysteries. A brilliantly funny and much-needed site!

When Toilets go Bad!

http://home.att.net/~toyletbowlbbs/toilets.htm

It's tragic but true, we don't want to hear about it – but we can't help ourselves. Read through news stories of what happens when 'Toilets go bad!'.

The Mother of All Excuses Page

http://members.tripod.com/Madtbone/

Divided into categories such as police, school, work, and breaking a date – this site offers a plethora of excuses. Perhaps you will want to submit your own gems.

The Love Calculator

http://www.lovecalculator.com

'Do you love me 85 per cent?' 'Oh, then do you love me 76 per cent?'. Enter two names into the Love Calculator and find out what your chances really are.

Tip a Cow

http://www.nwlink.com/~timelvis/cowtip.html

Real-life cow tipping is a dangerous and cruel prank – but at this site you can fulfill your desire to tip a virtual cow as many times as you like!

Interactive Heckler Page

http://www.hecklers.com

This site encourages your participation – the jokes and pranks are updated often, be sure to have a good browse around.

Python Online

http://www.pythononline.com/

The official site of all things relating to the pythonesque world of 'Monty Python'. An absolute must for fans.

Surfing Sobriety Test

http://www.turnpike.net/~mirsky/drunk/test1.html

Are you sober enough to be surfing the Net? Take this test to find out. Amongst other things, you will have to click on a picture of a nose with your eyes shut, and click across the screen in a straight line!

The Movie Nitpickers' Site

http://www.nitpickers.com/

We've all seen them – those continuity mistakes, the out-of-sequence scenes where the empty glass has become full. Here's the site where you can register your own movie nitpick, or just peruse the massive archive of what other people have already noticed.

Stare Down Sally

http://www.stairwell.com/stare/

Sally will blink...eventually! Do you think you're a match for her?

The Guy Card

http://www.guycard.com/

Do you feel your right to be a guy is diminished in this modern world? Do you want to reclaim the right to dress like a guy, watch guy TV and generally do guy things? If you answered 'Yes' to any of these questions, you obviously need a 'Guy Card'.

The Cyrano Server

http://www.nando.net/toys/cyrano/

Would you like to email a splendid literary masterpiece to a loved one, to let them know how much you care, even though you can't quite find the right words? Let the 'Cyrano Server' help you out!

Write Like an Egyptian

http://www.upenn.edu/museum/Collections/egyptian.html

This fantastic site will render your name or any other word you type on the form into colorful Egyptian hieroglyphs.

Purity Tests Online

http://www.armory.com/tests/

Purity Tests measure how 'pure' you are within some realm of experience and then give you a rating out of 100 per cent. This 'Adults Only' site lists a large number of Purity Tests that can be found online.

Pretty Strange Patents

http://soundreach.simplenet.com/psp

Peruse the archives to find out what people invent when they simply have too much spare time on their hands!

The Toilet Museum

http://www.toiletmuseum.com/

'Ladies' Room', 'Men's Room', 'The Great Outdoors', 'Technotoilet' – just some of the toilet information to be found at this site!

The Virtual Bachelor Pad

http://www.ziggyland.com

Visit the life of a bachelor! Peek inside the bachelor brain or tinker with the bachelor laundry system – if you dare!

Return of the Muppets

http://www.muppets.com

TV's top glove puppets review their favorite websites. Also, find out where Miss Piggy is whilst she's on tour!

Dog Years

http://www.patsyann.com/school/years.htm

This site makes calculation of the above very easy – you can sit there and calculate the dog years of your entire family!

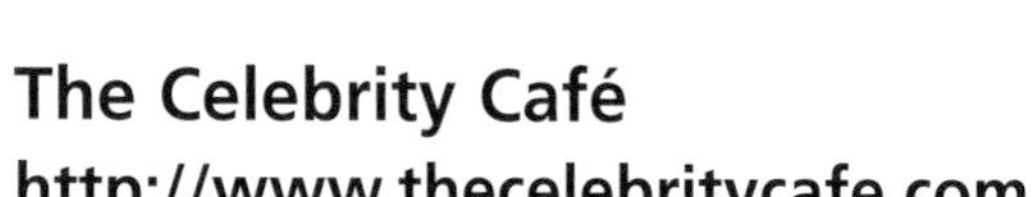

The Celebrity Café

http://www.thecelebritycafe.com

This online magazine features celebrity interviews, music reviews, travel stories, and more. Check it out!

Virtual Bubblewrap

http://fathom.org/opalcat/bubblewrap.html

We have all done it, popped those bubbles – but isn't it disappointing when they are all popped? Well, here you can find virtual bubblewrap, which you can pop forever!

The Virtual Bachelor Pad

http://www.ziggyland.com/

Visit the life of a bachelor! Peek inside the bachelor brain or tinker with the bachelor laundry system – if you dare!

Out-of-body Experiences

http://www.med.virginia.edu/personality-studies/

The University of Virginia explores case studies on this web site – including 'Out-of-body' occurrences and children who claim to remember previous lives.

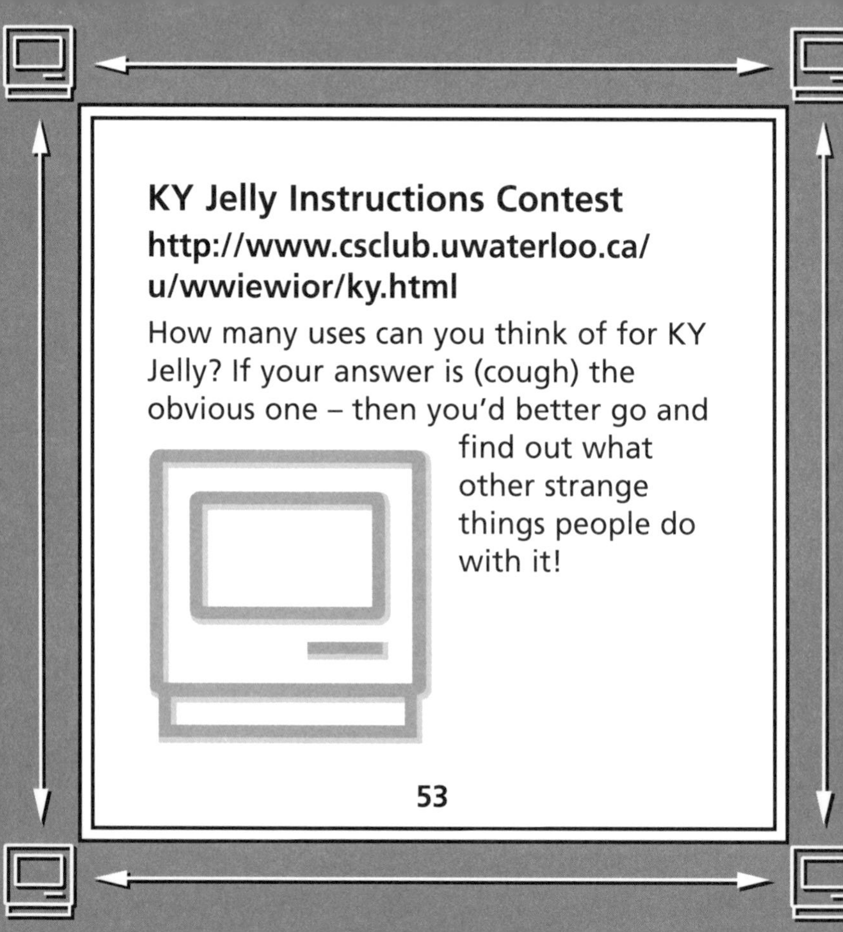

KY Jelly Instructions Contest

http://www.csclub.uwaterloo.ca/u/wwiewior/ky.html

How many uses can you think of for KY Jelly? If your answer is (cough) the obvious one – then you'd better go and find out what other strange things people do with it!

The Really Big Button That Doesn't Do Anything

http://www.pixelscapes.com/spatulacity/button.htm

You can argue with it, you can try it for yourself, you can see what others have to say about it. Go on, push it – you know you want to!

Find Your Star Wars Twin

http://www.outofservice.com/starwars/

Via a short personality test, you can find out if you too are intimately related to a personality featured in 'Star Wars'.

Hollywood Star Map!

http://www.geocities.com/RodeoDrive/2800/starmap.html

Find out where your favorite Hollywood stars live on this neat site. As well as the addresses, there are street maps and loads of photo galleries!

The Life of a Hair Ball

http://mypage.direct.ca/k/kbotham/hairyindex.html

The hilarious photo-documented story of the life of a hair ball…the tragedy…the joy…and the drain!

Fan Club Finder

http://members.aol.com/lknafc/nafc

Looking for the fan club for your favorite celebrity? Check out the extensive listings here. If you can't find the club you're looking for, e-mail the site with your request!

Who Wants To Be a Millionaire?

http://www.themilliondollar.com/

Buy your very own million dollar bill for just $0.45.

Celebrity Websites

http://www.celebrity-websites.com

Visit here to discover the unofficial web sites dedicated to a panoply of celebrities. There's loads to see here!

A Celeb on Your Desktop

http://www.celebritydesktop.com

Do you have a favorite celebrity? Then why not install him or her on your computer permanently as a screensaver or wallpaper? There are thousands of free downloads here, from Angelina Jolie to Michael Jackson!

The UFO Network

http://www.ufon.org

The UFO Network site charts UFO sightings from around the world. Check out the archive photos and decide for yourself whether or not they are hoaxes.

Alien Research

http://users.erols.com/feanor17/Ufo.html

Apparently aliens have been meddling in our affairs since before the dawn of intelligence on this planet. Read the evidence here.

Film Flaws

http://www.moviecliches.com/

Listed by topic, this fab web site contains the most common and annoying celluloid clichés. 'Bombs' is my favorite – what's yours?

Give the Gift of...?

http://www.nothing.net/nothing/index.html

What do you give the person who has everything? The answer is 'nothing'! This site has details about why 'nothing' makes a fabulous gift.

The Robot Store

http://www.robotstore.com/

Do you want to build a kit robot? This online store might be the place for you to start.

Make His Day

http://www.clinteastwood.net

Sashay over to the web site of one of Hollywood's top actors and directors, Clint Eastwood. You can download film clips, music recordings, still photos, and even a message for your telephone answering machine!

The Morse Code Translator

http://www.urban75.com/Mag/morse.html

This site is almost totally useless unless, of course, you've always wanted to translate lots of things into morse code.

April Fools Online

http://www.wonderfullywacky.com

Don't know what to buy your boring aunt or uncle? Make their day with a Kung Fu Hamster, Moose Poop Candy Dispenser or Chocolate Body Painting Kit. Priceless (but yours for just $44.95).

Alien Abductions Inc.

http://www.alienabductions.com/

Feeling left out in the abduction stakes? Wonder why aliens haven't picked you up yet? This funny site offers 'genuine' abduction memory implants – out of this world!

Useless Facts Page

http://www.uselessfacts.net

Useless facts it promises and useless facts it gives, by the wagon-load. They're arranged in 18 different categories from 'Animals & Creatures' to 'Statistics', and the criterion used for selection is, if it's funny it must be true!

The Death Clock

http://www.deathclock.com

Plug your details into the 'Death Clock' and let it tell you how long you've got to go!

One Potato, Two Potato...

http://www.readingtoes.com

Your toes may reveal more about you than you realize. Get the lowdown here from the official web site of the Foundation for Fundamental Dactylogical Reading.

Laugh Till You Cry

http://www.bigpuns.com

Groan over the latest puns from Punmaster Dan, or peruse past gems in the archives. No more, please, my sides are splitting!

Reverse Speech

http://www.reversespeech.com/

This fascinating site explains Reverse Speech Technology and offers real audio examples of famous people's speeches played backwards!

The Haunting of Wil's Apartment

http://www.wilwa.net/wil/

Wil, a writer and former skeptic, has created this site – complete with detailed diary entries and a map of his haunted apartment.

The Vegetable Rights Association

http://www.village.org/bvra/Welcome.html

Strike a blow against herbivores everywhere – speak up for the greens!

Web of Lies

http://www.cs.man.ac.uk/~hancockd/lies.htm

There are nearly 4,000 lies at this site – from women are 12 times more radioactive than men to Scotch Tape will only work if you are a Scot (otherwise it just pretends). Unbelievable!

The World of Unicorns

http://www.geocities.com/Area51/Corridor/5177

This site offers art, quotes, and links about the mythical beast – you can even adopt your very own unicorn here!

Live Better, Live Cheaper

http://www.stretcher.com

Even if you think you're good with money, this page 'for professional tightwads' could be a real eye-opener. Read tips here about how to live better for less, and contribute your own.

The Cat Scan Contest

http://www.cat-scan.com/

Sometimes you have to take the name literally! The Cat Scan Contest is a hilarious contest to find the best photo of a scanned cat! Check it out!

TV Eyes

http://www.tveyes.com/

This incredible site offers to email you when a word of your choosing is spoken on television – why don't you try it for yourself.

Peeping Tom

http://www.coolbase.com/peepingtom/index.html

The site has links to web-cams in cities around the world. Get someone to wave to you…then go take a look!

Ask Bob!

http://www.resort.com/~banshee/Misc/8ball/index.html

Facing a tough decision? The mystical smoking head of Bob is here to help you. Just enter your question, and wait for the oracle to answer in a puff of pipe smoke!

The Annual Leisure Suit Convention

http://desires.com/1.4/Style/Docs/leisure.html

Did you really think that leisure suits and their owners were extinct? Think again!

Ghost Towns

http://www.ghosttowngallery.com

Are you fascinated by the images of ghost towns in old movies, with their abandoned buildings and drifting tumbleweed? Yes? Then this site's for you!

Dancing Paul

http://www.dancingpaul.com

Watch 'Cool Paul' dance to a selection of top disco tracks. You can even choose the scenery in the background!

The Amazing 'Send Me a Dollar' Web Site

http://server.tt.net/send-me-a-dollar/

It's amazing what people use the Internet for. Give this guy a medal! Check out how many dollars he has already accumulated – you won't believe it.

The Death Test

http://test.thespark.com/deathtest/

Fill in the details and cringe or alternatively celebrate the results! How long have you got left?

Ultimate Taxi

http://www.ultimatetaxi.com

Why bother catching a cab to go to the local nightclub when the cab is the nightclub, complete with glitter ball and disco lights. Space is limited though – not for the John Travoltas of this world I fear!

The Incredible World of Navel Fluff

http://www.feargod.net/fluff.html

How much belly-button fluff do you think one person can collect in a jar in a year? This site claims to show you the record-holder. Useful, eh?

The Dark Side of Scooby Doo

http://www.cdc.net/~drjekyll/scooby/darkside/

Finally someone has seen through the disguise – visit this site to view the alter-egos of Scooby, Scrappy, Velma, Freddy and Daphne.

3

Food and Drink

Iron Liver

http://www.mit.edu.8001/activities/btb_tml/drinks.html

If you are brave enough to attempt mixing and then drinking the concoction that appears on this site, you're either a hardened drinker or a cyborg!

Foodoo

http://www.foodoo.co.uk

Like to eat but refuse to spend hours slaving over a hot stove? Foodoo's tips and recipes will make your culinary life easy.

Green Power

http://www.ivu.org

This one-stop shop for vegetarians is full of health tips and nutrition issues to keep you fighting fit and perky.

Beer for Boffins

http://www.beerinfo.com

From real ale to a six-pack with your buddies, this site is a must for all beer lovers.

Cocktail

http://www.hotwired.com/cocktail

No, it won't turn you into Tom Cruise, but you will learn how to mix an extra dry martini to satisfy James Bond himself.

Virtual Blender

http://www.hotwired.com/cocktail

Visit the alchemist, try the drink of the week, and learn the art of mixology at this fruity and potent site for cocktail lovers everywhere.

Chopstix

http://www.chopstix.co.uk

Chinese food fans will love this site, filled with recipes and articles, plus lots of advice to stop you getting your chopsticks in a twist.

Food Frenzy

http://www.zagart.com

Want Thai in Sydney and Moroccan in New York? Then visit the site that features reviews of restaurants in over 30 cities worldwide.

Food Fodor

http://www.fodors.com/ri.cgi

You may have seen their travel guides, and now Fodor have an online restaurant guide too. Here it is, listed by priced sections to help you keep the pennies!

Global Kitchen

http://www.globalgourmet.com

For gluttons and gourmets alike – find the origin of your favorite food and grab a few excellent and easy-to-follow recipes at this culinary site.

Simply Food

http://www.simplyfood.com

Plan your next dinner party with the aid of tips and recipes featured at this well-designed site.

Mistress of the Cake

http://www.bettycrocker.com

She is a national treasure and this rich site is full of her ideas, easy-to-prepare recipes and cooking tips for every occasion.

Le Gourmet

http://www.frenchwinesfood.com

There are hardly any low-fat recipes at this French cuisine site – so stop living on lettuce and take your tastebuds on an odyssey of French food.

Junior Kitchen

http://www.yumyumskitchen.com

Remember being allowed to lick the spoon after the cake was mixed when you were a kid? Well, kids now have the opportunity to make their own kiddie-sized cakes here!

French Foodie

http://thefoodweb.com

The home of great food ideas, this site includes everything from food debate to hangover cures, and includes your favorite TV chefs.

The Holy Grape

http://www.winespectator.com

If you have a love of fine wine but want an appreciation of it, grab your corkscrew and check out this web site – you'll come away with an in-depth knowledge.

Daily Wine

http://www.dailywine.com

Log on daily to see which lucky wine has been nominated 'wine of the day' – the suspense is intense!

Wine Lovers

http://www.wine-lovers-page.com

Wine lovers from around the globe, rejoice, for this is your new home! Not only does this site review fine wines, it welcomes your say at their forum too.

Dean and Deluca

http://www.deananddeluca.com

Direct from a stylish deli in New York, this site of top class food will make you drool all over your keyboard!

Spice Guide

http://www.spiceguide.com

Do you panic with paprika or lack confidence with coriander? Then check out this spice site to learn what goes well with what and how to pep up your culinary expertise.

Food, Glorious Food

http://food.epicurious.com

A one-stop shop where every conceivable brand, type and combination of food is revealed – it features over 10,000 recipes and is updated daily!

5,000 Ways

http://www.idrink.com

An informative site regarding the mixing of alcoholic spirits…it lists over 5,000 ways to damage your liver!

Kosher

http://www.kashrusmagazine.com/

If you eat kosher food, you will be excited to find a site that has a great choice and availability of chosen foods for you.

Three Fat Chicks

http://www.3fatchicks.com

Join the three fat chicks and watch your waistline. Great low fat recipes and nutritional advice found here will help you win the battle of the bulge.

Recipe Exchange

http://www.recipexchange.com

Send your tried-and-tested recipes to other global gluttons to inflict on their loved ones. You won't believe what some people put on their pizza!

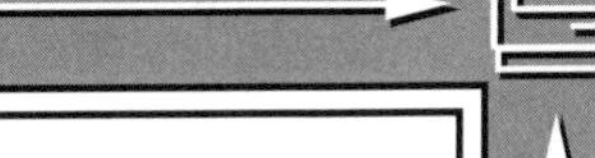

Spice It Up!

http://www.spiceadvice.com

From allspice to vanilla, everything you need to know about where they come from, what to put them in, and recipes that include them.

Vodka Vamps

http://www.stoli.com

A fun and funky site dedicated to the world domination by this king of spirits.

Organics

http://www.organicsdirect.com

Organic food can sometimes be hard to come by, so if you would like to sign up for an organic food delivery service, check out this splendid network of links.

Juicy Meat

http://www.meatmatters.com

It was out of fashion but is now back with a vengeance, so get on this meaty site filled to the brim with recipes and nutritional advice.

Cyber Veg

http://www.vegweb.com

Veggies usually get the thin end of the carrot when it comes to recipes and cooking, but this vitamin-enriched site puts vegetarians firmly on center stage with tips and recipes.

Good Pub Guide

http://www.goodguides.com/

Any visitor to Britain is usually keen to check out the pub culture – so enjoy it in your very own home with this cyber guide to cozy pubs, good beer and home-cooking.

Dinner Party Hell

http://www.mealsforyou.com

Take the stress and swearing out of entertaining by viewing this helpful UK-based site. You'll never panic again when your other half announces the boss is turning up for dinner!

Chocolate Playground

http://www.godiva.com

Fantastic hot and bubbly chocolate site – wander the historical halls of cocoa history and satisfy your sweetest cravings!

Dante's Ninth Circle

http://www.kidsparties.com

Children's parties can be hell! But these US party experts have provided online tips about food and entertainment, so all you have to worry about is the clearing up later!

All and Everything

http://www.allrecipes.com

This US-based cookery site features recipes for every occasion – from breakfast through to midnight munchies. You need never be hungry!

Party Food

http://www.geocities.com/paris/leftbank/2710/menu.html

Drink and music may be the basis of a good party but the food needs to be pretty special too! For a party your guests will never forget, this web site provides free catering advice.

Shake It All About

http://www.cocktailsearch.com

From the classics to the latest trends, this site tells you all you need to know about your favorite mixed drinks and cocktails.

I'll Have a Bottle of...

http://latour/home.html

There's nothing worse than being unable to pronounce wine names in restaurants – so this amazing site contains sound files on pronunciation to help spare your blushes!

What's for Dinner?

http://www.recipe-a-day.com

Don't make a mountain out of meal times! – Simply visit here and they will serve you a delicious fresh recipe each and every day.

Blindin' Food Mate!

http://www.bbc.co.uk/cgi-bin/food/recipes/search.pl?TYPE=2&CHEF=6

Get into the spirit with the naked chef Jamie Oliver and try his pukka recipes.

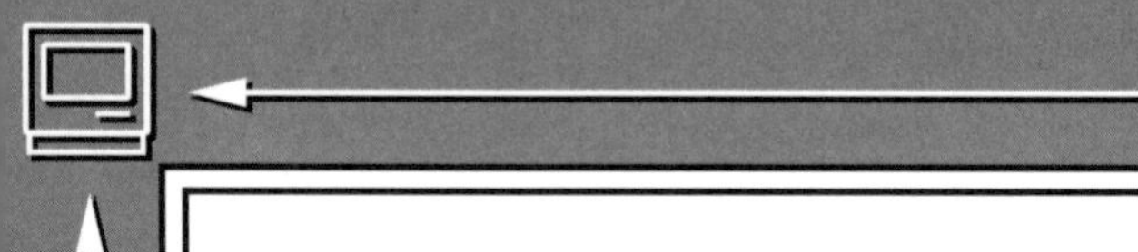

Beer Collectors

http://ourworld.compuserve.com/homepages/John_Mann/abbchome.htm

Some people collect matchboxes or vintage cars…and some collect beer bottles! Log on to the Association of Bottled Beer Collectors' web site if you wish to join too!

Recipe Source

http://www.recipesource.com

Browse by region or type of dish on this vast international site to find the perfect mouth-watering dish for every occasion.

Moonshine

http://www.lusionspub.com

Imagine how much money you would save if you knew how to make your own quality spirits and liqueurs! Well, follow the free recipes here and brew up a storm.

Worldwide Hampers

http://www.worldwide-hampers.com

At this palate-tempting site you can order a vast array of organic food, wine, flowers and gifts to make that special someone's day!

Edible Insects

http://www.eatbug.com

Two words meant to be put together? Visit this site and then decide for yourself as they try to convince you that bugs are low in fat and high in protein.

Fax Fruit

http://www.cityfruits.com/

Not literally of course! But you can order a fruit basket for a friend at this online store. And if they're not a friend – how about sending a big raspberry?

Bar Meister

http://www.barmeister.com

Featuring the top ten drinks of the day, you'll never get caught out serving a 'Cosmopolitan' instead of a 'Juicirene' again!

Star Chefs

http://www.starchefs.com

Chefs are the new media darlings, and at this web site you will find articles and tips from the very cream of the crop.

Cooking Index

http://www.cookingindex.com

Mary Jane has dedicated her life to finding the best the web has to offer on cooking, kitchen and diet-related links – log on and don't disappoint her!

Possum Cookbook

http://www2.msstate.edu/~brb1/possum.html

Catch 'em, kill 'em, and eat 'em! – all the recipes and tips about eating what most people traditionally think of as roadkill!

Cyber Kitchen

http://home.achilles.net/~sscrruton/comfort.html

Nothing beats a little bit of comfort and self indulgence – and here is where you will find delicious recipes to soothe your soul.

Soda Fountain

http://www.tasteofthepast.com/

Revisit a bygone age and learn the history of your favorite drinks and the location of the nearest 'Soda Fountain' to you.

Easy Eats

http://www.meals.com

You get home, you're tired, and you want a quick, easy-to-prepare meal – visit this site for instant recipes and add them to your personalized online cookbook for next time.

Anyone for Coffee?

http://www.whittard.com

This London Chelsea-based company specializes in specialty teas and coffee – impress the neighbors by ordering a selection and expertly serving it according to their step-by-step instructions.

Cook's Thesaurus

http://www.foodsubs.com/

Know your bergamots from your calamondins at this cooking encyclopedia web site that includes descriptions and pronunciations of many ingredients and kitchen tools.

Culinary Café

http://www.culinarycafe.com

Cooking will never be a chore again at the culinary café that provides recipes for everything from barbecue food to vegetable dishes.

Cheese Lover

http://www.cheese.com

You won't believe the number and variety of cheese featured at this cheesefest of a site – they even offer to publish your favorite cheese recipes.

Food Channel

http://www.foodchannel.com

Crammed full of articles on topical food issues such as raising vegetarian children and new food web sites, this site also has quizzes and polls to keep you amused.

Turning Japanese

http://bento.com/tokyofood.html

This Tokyo food page is a complete guide to Japanese cuisine – they even tell you how to co-ordinate your interiors to match your favorite sushi variety!

Hail Caesar Salad!

http://www.mit.edu/people/wchuang/cooking/recipes/Roman

Try something different and create some exotic dishes from ancient Rome, or you'll be thrown to the lions!

Top Secret!

http://www.topsecretrecipes.com

Sssh! Here you will discover the secret recipes to your favorite fast food. How many secret herbs and spices were there again?

French Gourmet

http://www.jayfruit.com

This smart online store can bring tantalizing French delicacies straight to your door – choose from the likes of truffles, caviar and crustacea.

Kitchen Link

http://www.kitchenlink.com

Your online guide to what's cooking on the Net. This site features recipes, online chat, and a message board to help you keep in touch with other food lovers.

Food Tech

http://www.foodbiotech.org

This informative site offers serious general info on food biotechnology, and features industry news and regional experts for the serious food enthusiast.

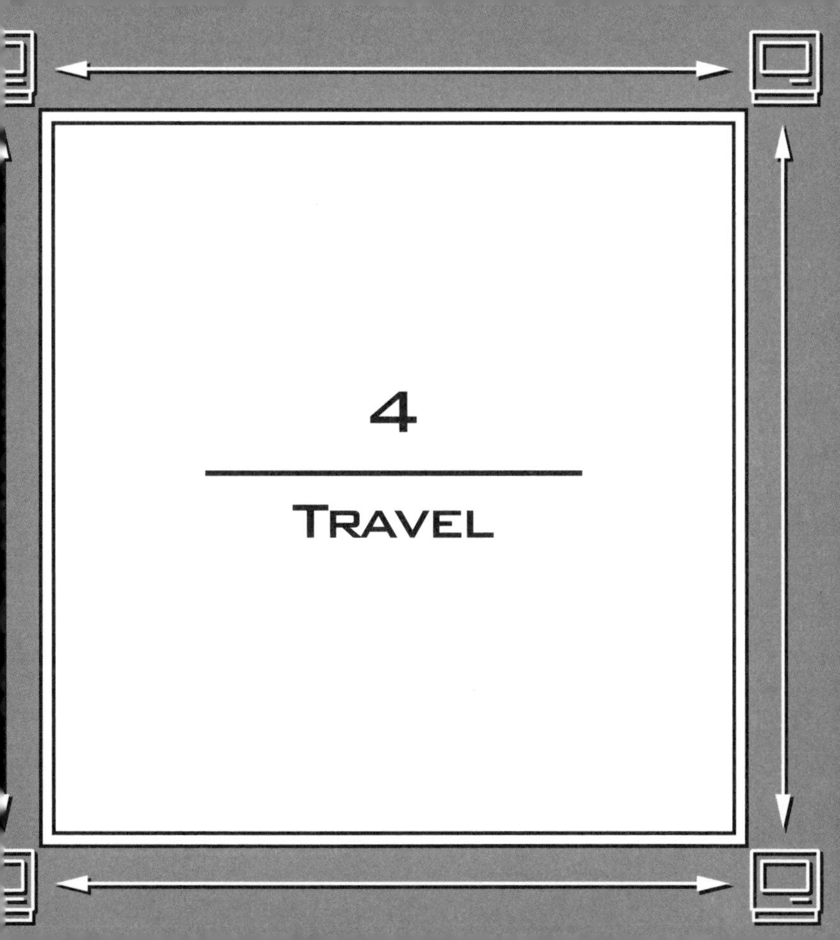

4

Travel

Bargains Galore

http://www.bargainholidays.com

If you're broke but in need of a holiday, this is the site for you! It's full of terrific bargains for the perfect getaway!

Down Mexico Way

http://www.go2mexico.com

This site, dedicated to the charms of Mexico, is very well researched and will make you want to dive into the screen!

Euro-tastic!

http://www.theeuroguide.com/2002/index.html

Heading for Europe? Then check out this cultural guide to popular events and venues in Paris, Brussels and beyond!

Fly Cheap

http://www.cheapflights.com

This does what it says, which is to scour the Web for the cheapest flights possible – spend time here and save money!

Christine Columbus

http://www.christinecolumbus.com

Great site for independent female travelers that is full of travel advice, such as leave one-third of your luggage at home and photocopy your passport!

World Info

http://www.travel-guides.com

This site provides practical info on every single country in the world. A great global one-stop travel shop.

City Guide

http://www.cnn.com/TRAVEL/

Save yourself sore feet and plan ahead by downloading a map of the city you are about to visit.

Out of Africa

http://www.africaguide.com

Planning a trip to Africa? Then here is a factual site with details on safaris, sights and, most importantly, sound medical advice.

Virtual Eire

http://www.goireland.com

You've celebrated St Patrick's Day every year and have drunk Guinness yet still don't know the real Ireland, so plan a trip via this green site.

Sound Advice

http://www.thebackpacker.net

If you're the type who takes each day as it comes on holiday, then keep the useful tips on this site in the back of your mind.

Get Here Quick

http://www.gettinghere.com

Filled with exotic destination guides to Asia and the Far East plus helpful service and travel guides, you will definitely want to get there quick!

Travelling Underbelly

http://www.underbelly.com/index.html

No, not a cure for Delhi Belly, but a very useful reality check on some of the things that the brochures won't always tell you!

Fodors

http://www.fodors.com

The destination for any destination, Fodor's classic site provides trip ideas, bargains and expert advice for both novice and experienced travelers.

Multimap

http://www.multimap.com

Travelling around a new country can be difficult and dangerous if you don't know where you are going, so let Multimap take away the hassle.

Alien Holiday

http://www.alienabductions.com

If your idea of a great holiday is to be whisked off into the solar system, this is a great place to find out what your chances are of being grabbed by little green men!

Customs

http://www.customs.treas.gov

Check the US customs requirements of the country you are visiting before you arrive at this useful site, so there won't be any unforeseen dramas when you get there.

Underwater Aviation

http://www.deepflight.com

You may mock, but once you have your 'underwater aviation certificate' the world is your oyster! Build your own customized U-boat and discover Atlantis!

Off the Tourist Track

http://www.straytravel.com

Log on here for an amazing off-the-beaten-track way to experience the best that Europe, Britain and Ireland have to offer.

iCircle

http://www.icircle.com/travel

Aimed at female travelers, discover tips and advice on safety, top destinations, and everything else in between.

How Far?

http://www.indo.com/distance

Log on to calculate the exact distance from city to city – did you know that it's only 16,997 kilometers from London to Sydney?

On Expenses

http://www.biztravel.com

You've talked your boss into a large expense account for that trip to Florida – visit here to make those dollars go even further!

Trail Mail

http://www.trailmail.com

This excellent site lets your friends and family know where you are and what you've been doing – just register your details and write your travel journal online, so your family can log on to read your news!

Camel Expert

http://www.1001sites.com

Check out this brilliant site containing vast amounts of info on Arab countries, their history, culture and invaluable travel tips.

Virgin Traveler

http://www.virgin.net

A well-polished site that gives you all the info you need to plan your break away, from currency to weather and world maps.

Global Buddy

http://www.netcafeguide.com

While you're away, don't forget the people left behind – find out how to stay in touch at this site and keep your mom happy!

Last Minute

http://www.lastminute.com

For those who like to fly off to far-flung destinations at a moment's notice, then this UK site full of last minute deals was designed with you in mind!

On the Trot

http://www.tripprep.com

Have a healthy adventure and check out this travel health site before you go. Learn how to avoid exotic diseases and the distressing digestive disorders!

Cam on Sydney

http://www.viewsydney.com

If you are considering going 'down under', you may want to take a peek at what's in store by logging on this web-cam view facing Sydney Harbor.

There's No Place Like Home

http://www.cybercafe.com

Need to send an email home in a hurry? Then check out this database directory of over 4,200 Internet café addresses in 148 different countries.

Tractor Travel

http://www.ytmag.com

You'll definitely be noticed if you travel in this convertible – click on to this fun site and check out the uncoolest way to travel!

Travel Under Water

http://www.eurostar.com

A fast and user-friendly site, that helps if you're planning a trip to France or Belgium from England – check out the Eurostar travel times and book tickets online.

Student Travel

http://www.sta.com

If you are under 26 or still studying, this online travel agency will find great travel deals and give you some helpful tips too!

My Right!

http://www.passengerrights.com

When something doesn't go to plan on holiday, you can often feel quite helpless, so log on here to find out about your rights in case you need to register a complaint.

Where Will We Go?

http://www.wherewillwego.com

Stuck for ideas on where to go for your next vacation? Simply choose the continent, country and type of holiday here, and they'll do the rest for you. Easy!

Tulips from Amsterdam

http://www.channels.nl

Visit Amsterdam for its art and culture – and, of course, the tulips! Here you will find expert tips and travel advice.

Bumper B&B

http://www.innsite.com

Need cheap accommodation while travelling but don't want to get to know the cockroaches? – this enormous database of short-stay places will be a great help.

Bidding War!

http://priceline.com

You register here how much you're prepared to pay for an international ticket from anywhere in the US and wait to see if someone is prepared to accept it. Easy!

Walk Like an Egyptian

http://www.touregypt.net

Explore the ancient world of Pharaohs and mummies – not to mention the inspirational pyramids – at the official Egyptian tourism site.

My Journal

http://www.travel-library.com

Share your adventures with fellow travelers and benefit from their experience by logging on to this 'travel library', which allows you to receive the latest news from other people doing the same trip as you!

Hong Kong

http://www.discoverhongkong.com/

It may be a shopper's paradise, but there is more to Hong Kong than designer handbags. This sparkling site will give you the latest info on culture and accommodation.

Destination Adrenalin

http://www.comebackalive.com/df/

If all you usually risk on holiday is sun burn, get on this site, which will arrange a heart-thumping holiday of a lifetime for you!

Virtual Tourist

http://www.vtourist.com

Act like a native and confidently jump on buses, underground systems and trams in foreign cities. Just view this great site that allows you to map out your journey beforehand.

Flowers in Your Hair

http://www.hotelres.com

San Francisco – the trams, the Golden Gate bridge, the hills – discover why this city is so popular and book accommodation online here.

Flamenco Fun

http://www.spaintour.com

Visit this sizzling site to see why you should be visiting Spain! Soak up the culture and sunshine online!

Shoestring Oz

http://www.ozexperience.com

Imagine camping out under the stars, seeing the Sydney Opera House, and traveling through the bush – well, now you can with this online budget travel network.

Passage to India

http://www.iloveindia.com

If you want to see what you're missing out on, take a walk through this magical site dedicated to the amazing country of India.

Ciao Bella!

http://www.initaly.com

An invaluable research site on the wonderful land of Italy, covering art, food, culture and practical advice for would-be tourists.

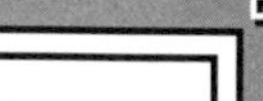

Romantic Break

http://www.paris-touristoffice.com

It's impossible not to love Paris and you will be totally seduced at a site that allows you to take a virtual stroll through this most romantic of cities.

Go West!

http://www.istc.org

Still a student? Then sign up to this online discount travel scheme and enjoy cut-price deals to major destinations.

Rat Race

http://www.i-to-i.com

Escape the rat race and have some fun doing voluntary work abroad. There are over 300 projects here for you to choose from so open your eyes to a real world experience.

Thelma and Louise

http://www.journeywoman.com

Excellent ezine for real 'Thelma and Louise' girls – you don't have to be on the run, just visit here for girl-friendly city spots advice and hot tips on safety.

City of Angels

http://www.la.com

If you are thinking about discovering, or being discovered in, Los Angeles then check out this celebrity-packed site for the latest on traveling around and entertainment.

Time Travel

http://www.timeanddate.com

You'll need to know what time it is at the place you will be visiting, so you don't ring home in the middle of the night.

Earth-Cam

http://www.earthcam.com

Need to know the weather in Africa or the traffic in New York? This site has cams all over the world to give you vital up-to-date info and statistics.

Caribbean Fever

http://www.caribtravelnews.com

Roll out your towel, slap on sunscreen, and sip a cool cocktail as you click on to this chilled site all about paradise on earth!

Ski Heaven

http://www.1ski.com

This online guide contains everything from snow reports, events and resort guides to make your ski holiday truly enjoyable.

Points Mean Prizes

http://www.frequentflier.com

Start saving now and you could, one day, fly free to New Zealand! This site lists the participating airlines and their point schemes – only 20,000 to go!

House Swap

http://www.homexchange.com

If you can bear the thought of a stranger in your bathtub, why not take a cheap holiday by swapping homes through this online agency?

Prego!

http://www.travlang.com

Need to ask for two cappuccinos in Italy or want to learn a new foreign word or phrase each day? Then log on to this database for all your foreign language needs.

Accidental Tourist

http://www.strolling.com

Sometimes it's hard to get time to have a weekend break, so pull up your armchair and take a virtual stroll through New York without so much as a blister!

Life at Sea

http://www2.i-cruise.com/

For that special occasion or for a holiday with a difference, why not take a cruise? This informative site will tell you all the facts you need to know.

No Money, No Problem

http://www.artoftravel.com

Having only a little money is no excuse not to see the world at this web site, which reveals how you can see it all for only $25 a day!

Viva Las Vegas

http://www.insidervlv.com/elvis

It's loud, brash and tacky – and you shouldn't miss it for the world! Log on to find out all about the glitz and glamor that is Las Vegas.

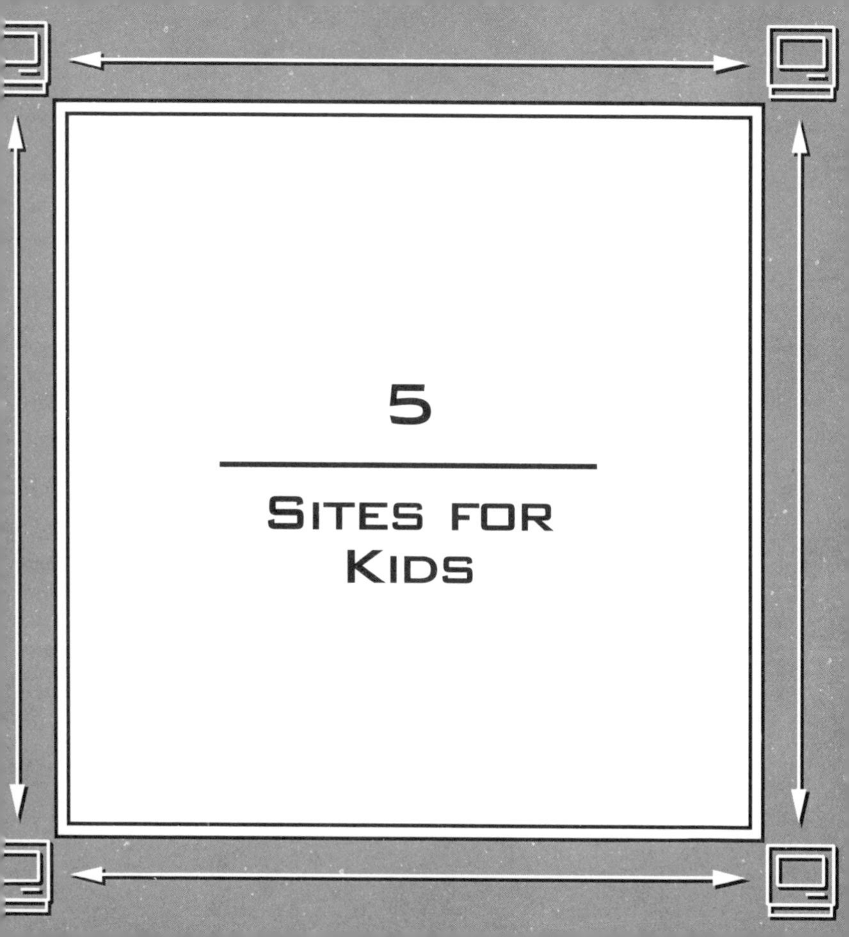

5

Sites for Kids

Harry Potter Land

http://harrypotter.warnerbros.com/

Everything you need to know about the young hero of wizardry, Hogwarts and all. Read about his adventures and catch up on the latest info about the boy genius.

Teenz Rule!

http://www.cyberteens.com/ctmain.html

Billed as the Internet's Number One online community for the world's youth, this site features art and stories – you can even submit your own work.

Wacky Web Tales

http://www.eduplace.com/tales

Choose from a list of story titles like 'Burp!' and 'Goaaa!' Fill in the form with your own words. Then sit back and giggle as your words are used to fill in the blanks to create a story of serious strangeness.

Welcome to Seussville!

http://www.randomhouse.com/kids/

The cat in the hat talks back! Visit the Seussville University and have fun with all your favorite Dr Seuss characters.

Keypal

http://www.kidscom.com/orakc/pwdkeypal.html

Find a friend with similar interests and chat live with other kids. There's also a graffiti wall! 'Kidscom' monitors the chat and your parents' permission is required.

How Stuff Works

http://www.howstuffworks.com

If you've ever been awake at night wondering how planes fly, 'How Stuff Works' lives up to its name and explains how anything works.

Garfield's Great

http://www.garfield.com

He's a crazy, lovable, orange cat and this is his site, jam-packed with book reviews, comics, fun and games.

Wired for Sound

http://www.niehs.nih.gov/kids/music.htm

Simply select a song from well over 100 in the 'Children's' list link, plug in your headphones, and listen to your favorites in super stereo.

Celebrity Pics

http://www.yahooligans.com/Downloader/Pictures/Entertainment/Actors_Actresses/

Download some cool pictures of your favorite movie stars, from Ben Affleck to Kate Winslet.

My Story's on TV

http://www.storystudio.com/

If you want to write for TV, here's your chance. Submit a story to this show that dramatizes stories written by 10–14 year olds.

Boys Quest

http://www.boysquest.com

Learn how to make a solar-powered pocket watch, how to write a computer program, and some fun knot-tying tricks at this ezine that separates the men from the boys.

Hamster Dance

http://www.hamsterdance.com

Riverdance for rodents! There's a whole screenful of the little critters, complete with catchy soundtrack!

Fantasy T-shirts

http://www.smallfaces.com

This creative T-shirt company had the neat idea of T-shirts decorated with the torso of a fantasy character and you provide the 'head'! There are over 30 great designs to choose from!

Just Write

http://www.justwrite.org

Does the next 'Booker Prize' have your name on it? Start scribbling your poems and stories now and then submit them here for other kids to read and enjoy.

Adopt-a-pet

http://www.irwintoy.com/ MicroSite/default.asp

Click on your favorite toy to reveal a world of fun, games, and news. If you're feeling kinda crafty, you can join the Beadalicious Babes!

Peanuts Party

http://www.snoopy.com

This is the home of 'Peanuts' on the Web and there are trivia quizzes, coloring books, cartoons, and a 'Who's Who' of all the TV characters to keep you happy for hours.

Global Gang

http://www.globalgang.org.uk

Join the 'Global Gang' and find out about the lives of children in other parts of the world, as well as a ton of news, games, gossip and fun to keep you amused.

Magic Kat

http://www.frontiernet.net/~jackson/magickat.htm

If you want to see 'Magic Kat' pull a bear out of his hat, check out this fun animated magic show for kids of all ages.

Preppy Dresser or Surfer Dude?

http://www.teenvoice.com/Magnifique/Beauty/guysfashion.html

This cool fashion guide has put together several affordable looks to help you get to grips with your inner-style guru.

Gizmo Crafts

http://www.makestuff.com/kidstuff.html

There is a huge range of gizmos and gadgets for you to make here, including 'Film Cannister Rockets' and 'Body Tracing'. It's fun, easy and cheap, so what are you waiting for?

Speak Klingon!

http://www.kli.org/

If you have a passion for cool 'Klingon' speak, or just want to pick up a few words, check out 'the fastest growing language in the galaxy'.

Future Gadgets

http:/cbc4kids.ca/general/time/millenium/gadgets.html

What new gizmos will be essential to us in the not-too-distant future? Log on here to find out – there's loads here!

Personal Web Page

http://www.smplanet.com/webpage/webpage.htm

It's a lot simpler than it looks – in seven easy steps, this great site shows you everything you need to know about creating a web page.

Face Facts

http://www.facefacts.com

The face facts home is 'packed wall-to-wall with acne information'. Email a doctor from the privacy of the 'bedroom'; go to the 'kitchen' to check out the facts and myths surrounding greasy food; or look at pimple remedies in the 'bathroom'.

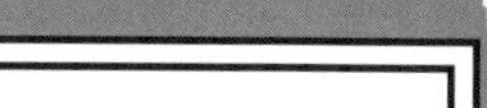

Cyber Cards

http://www.bluemountain.com

Forgotten a friend's birthday? Cyber your way back into their good books by sending a free personalized card. You can add a voice message and an optional personal message as well.

Virtual Pet Homepage

http://www.virtualpet.com/vp/

You can download and care for practically any pet, from a low-maintenance hamster or fish to the biggest dog you can find, at this site!

Movie Reporter

http://www.dove.org/MovieReporter/dovereviews.htm

Want to know if the latest movies are hot or not? Well here are the latest reviews on all your favorites including 'Lord of The Rings' and 'Harry Potter'.

Spy Kids

http://www.thefilmfactory.co.uk/spykids/frameset.htm

Infiltrate the spy academy to learn about the plot and characters of this hit family film.

Adventure Kit

http://www.adventurekit.com

Hit the wilderness trail and check out the survival gadgets and gizmos at this site. There's everything you can imagine from photon micro-lights to V7 watches.

Feeling Spacy?

http://www.holodeck3.com

The 'Star Trek' Holodeck is known as one of the best sites on the Net. Log on, choose where you want to work, and then …'Beam me up, Scotty'!

Games Paradise

http://www.gamesparadise.com

Wonder where all the kids at school find out about the latest computer games? Chances are, it is at this fantastic site!

Run Around Sioux

http://www.powwows.com/dancing

Don't be a Sitting Bull. Learn how to pow-wow and try out some Native-American dances like 'The Buckskin Wiggle', 'The Fancy Feather' and 'The Jingle'.

B-Boing!

http://www.bboy.com/break/moves.html

Yo! Breakdance like a pro. With a six-step lesson to funky popping, you can learn the lingo and the moves online!

Swing Out

http://www.swingmoves.com

Need a cheat sheet to work out the fancy footwork? Check out the dance moves on screen, then print it out!
If you want to swing but you ain't got that thing, then get some clout and check it out.

Boys' Toys

http://www.big-boys-toys.net/acatalog/index.html

Think James Bond at this online store that has a huge range of electrical equipment, extreme sports equipment, plus models and radio-controlled gadgets.

Volleyball

http://www.volleyball.com

Hit the beach in style after you have checked out this great volleyball site, filled with info on where to play, how to play, the pros, and advice in 'Coach's Corner'.

Stomp Up the Volume

http://www.stomponline.com

What is stomping? Elephants having a tantrum? No – it's a 'movement of bodies, objects and sounds'. Stompers use everyday objects to make music (or a whole lot of noise!). Your parents probably won't agree, but get into that kitchen, rattle those pots and get stomping.

BetterBodz

http://www.betterbodz.com/kids.html

Learn all about the skeleton system that holds you together and the importance of muscles and how they work at this helpful sports site.

Aim & Fire

http://library.thinkquest.org/27344/heavy.htm

Known as the sport of champions, you can learn its history and how to play here. What are we talking about? – Why, archery of course!

Name That Game!

http://www.demauro.com/games.html

25 games to keep you entertained for hours – ranging from trivia, to maze games, to word games!

Galaxy-H

http://www.galaxy-h.gov.uk

This cool spaceship site is dedicated to keeping you healthy and safe. Visit the 'Recreation Zone' to find out if you are doing enough exercise, or the 'Learning Zone' for healthy food advice. Enjoy your journey!

Bird Splatter and Alien Brunch!

http://www.adveract.com/games/games.htm

Be a winged menace as you win points by splattering people's cars. Or have fun with the aliens who want to invade New York in time for brunch!

Backyard Olympics

http://family.go.com/parties/events/feature/famf88games

You and your family are sure to love all these backyard games that are perfect for the long summer evenings.

Flying Machines

http://www.earlychildhood.com/crafts/index.cfm?FuseAction=Craft&C=17

Learn how to make and fly your very own kite. Up, up and away!

Kidzworld

http://www.kidzworld.com/frameset/flo5.htm

This is a colorful and funky sports site just for kids, featuring articles on a huge mixture of your favorite sports. Read all the news and views here.

Do the Hokey Pokéy

http://www.geocities.com/Area51/Crater/4784/Pokeguide.html

If your life has gone to pieces because you can't catch a wild Pokémon, then you'll soon feel better here!

Arcade Parade

http://www.kidsdomain.com

You can find lots of fabulous free downloads in this cool arcade site. There are literally hundreds of your favorite characters from film and television to enjoy!

High-Tech Jinks

http://www.scholastic.com/kids/games.htm

At this high-tech site, you can play the 'Cyber Speak Quiz' and meet 'Captain Underpants'! The 'Harry Potter Challenge' quiz is also waiting for you!

No Mess, No Fuss!

http://www.mv.com/ipusers/paintball/game

Get cyber-splattered with paint at this amazing site – you can go watch the games or register to play yourself.

Ssh! – Secret Agents

http://www.thunk.com

If you want to become a secret agent, you'll need this special secret message site. Type in your message and be amazed as it's magically turned into complete gobbledygook! And for the 'Junior James Bond', you can get the scoop on how secret codes are really used.

Warning – This Site Is Fowl!

http://www.brianmichaelsdj.com/chicken.htm

If cool ain't your thing – then you can wing it with the Chicken Dance. Say goodbye to street cred as you follow the steps of the silliest dance ever!

Grammar Gorillas

http://www.funbrain.com

Make friends with the grammar gorillas and put the correct word in the right sentence, go 'Mathcar Racing' and play 'Spellaroo'. Great fun!

Fast Fun Snacks

http://www.geocities.com/Heartland/7997/funsnacks.htm

You'll find these wacky snacks a breeze. There are loads to choose from, like peanut butter chocolate apples and octopus sandwiches!

Build Your Own Volcano!

http://hometown.aol.com/ckckside/reports/volcanoes/vol1.htm

Build an exploding volcano with stuff you can find lying around the house. Yes, really!

4 Kids 2 Play

http://www.4kids2play.nl/eng

Play traditional games such as 'Memory', 'Tic Tac Toe', and 'Tangram' here, as well as some new and unusual ones, such as 'Hanoi Tower' and 'Watch Out'.

Create Your Own Alien

http://www.alienexplorer.com/createalien/home.html

Let Mr Ducker, the kooky science teacher, show you how to create your very own space creature. Loads of little green links to other alien sites!

Get On Board

http://www.androidpubs.com

Got $2,000,000 to spare? You too could go to Mars then on the holiday of a lifetime. Check out the groovy pics of your intergalactic destination!

Death-like Blasters

http://www.createafart.com

Embarrass all your friends by emailing customized bodily noises to them! Choose from Death-Like Blasters and Long Stinky Rippers!

Wall Street Whizz Kids

http://www.younginvestor.com

Learn how to be a cool cash dude and have fun investing money. Yes, really! Start with the basics and find out how to make your allowance grrrowww!

Marius's Cow Tipping Page

http://www.blueneptune.com/~maznliz/tipcow.shtml

If your burning ambition has been to tip a virtual cow, don't let anything stand in the way of your dream!

Clever Clogs

http://www.studyweb.com

It's like having a clever pal sitting next to you who knows all the answers! From 'Anatomy' to 'Zoology', this vast reference site will help you finish your homework.

U Rule School

http://www.youruleschool.com

This is the place where the students do exactly what they like! Get yourself a nickname, a locker, and run down those cyber halls to the 'Laugheteria' and the 'Yumnasium'.

6

SPORT

Bend Me, Shake Me

http://www.yoga.com

Forget the face-lift – this excellent yoga site will stretch you further than a piece of chewing gum!

Go Girl!

http://www.wsf.org.uk

Visit the Womens Sport Foundation for the latest girl-friendly features, events and sports news.

Stretch and Tone

http://www.stretch.com

Stretching is an essential part of overall fitness. It not only makes you feel good, but it also increases flexibility and muscle tone.

Mega Muscles

http://www.ivillage.com/fitness

Everything you need to start a fitness program – there are a whole team of experts who can help you with the tips and exercises you need to begin.

Turn Off That TV

http://www.greatoutdoors.com

Get outside in the fresh air by visiting a site that provides info on lots of outdoor activities and also contains fascinating articles and destination guides.

Hoist the Sail

http://www.ybw.com

A marine web site where you can buy boats and equipment online, as well as book sailing and boating holidays for all levels of experience.

Stress Bunny

http://www.teachhealth.com

Stress can prevent you reaching your fitness peak, so let this online doctor take you through some easy stress-relief exercises.

Boy Racer

http://www.racecar.co.uk

Download screensavers, savor the action pics, and become the race car fantasy champion at this site for racing fanatics.

Dr Squat

http://drsquat.com

This site features a thigh-busting regime from Weightlifter Man! It's tough and scary, but you'll never feel unhealthy again!

Faith Sloan's Site

http://www.frsa.com/bbpage.shtml

Bodybuilding boffins will love the gallery of sweaty contestants and there are also links to fan sites and competition results.

Snow Bunny

http://www.skiers.com

Great ski site that has resort reviews, a trip planner, and snow reports, all to encourage you to hit the slopes in a hurry.

Insomnia Site

http://www.sleepquest.com/

Find out how to cure insomnia and get some shut-eye at this informative site.

Sporting Life

http://www.sporting-life.com

Live the sporting life with this regularly updated ezine dedicated to all your favorite sports, including the latest matches and scores.

Six-Pack Anyone?

http://www.muscle-fitness.com

This is the only six-pack you need! Check out the step-by-step guide to take you from flab to fit.

Thrive Online

http://thriveonline.oxygen.com/fitness/

Log on to learn how to increase your fitness, eat well and keep tabs on your weight.

Be Strong!

http://www.global-fitness.com/strength/s_map.html

How strong are you? This site lists the muscles in your body and explains how to strengthen and maintain them.

Senior Citizen Alert!

http://www.thirdage.com

If you are 50 or over and concerned about your fitness levels, this site is full of sensible advice on staying healthy for longer.

Chick Fit!

http://www.women.com

This bulging site provides very useful advice on women's bodies and how to take care of them.

Gym Buddies

http://www.primusweb.com/fitnesspartner

Going to the gym alone can be hard, so take your laptop with you as this site will act as your fitness partner!

Let's Get Physical

http://www.self.com/

A healthy ezine that gives women the latest on fitness, nutrition, pregnancy and weight-loss.

How Long Have I Got?

http://www.youfirst.com

Find out how healthy you really are by taking this online 'Health Risk Assessment Test'.

A–Z Health

http://www.healthatoz.com

There are so many sites linked to this one that you will have no problem finding a solution to your health or fitness problem.

Weekly Health Check

http://www.yourhealth.com

Health topics are updated weekly here and you can gain greater insight into the world of fitness by checking it regularly.

Medscape

http://www.medscape.com

Once the territory of the medical profession, Medscape is now available to answer medical concerns and questions.

Healthy Ideas

http://www.healthyideas.com

Advice from online medics who happily dish out tips and share knowledge – all without an appointment!

http://www.sports.com

This site gives you the latest developments from the world of sport. Dip into match reports and explore results and statistics.

Quit!

http://www.quitsmokingsupport.com

Stop making excuses! This comprehensive site gives you the facts and support you need to give up the evil weed forever.

http://www.sportal.co.uk

Explore the latest news from the worlds of cricket, football, Formula 1, golf, horse racing, rugby league, rugby union and tennis.

Sporting Dudes!

http://www.infoplease.lycos.com/sports.html

This is one of the world's biggest sports reference sites – there is a fantastic fan club section and up-to-date statistics.

You've Got Mail

http://www.infobeat.com

You can throw away the sports section of your daily newspaper, as this web site will choose sports news for you and email it direct.

Sports Feed

http://www.sportsfeed.com

International sports news will be at your fingertips daily at this great site. All the scores, stories and headlines for you to enjoy.

Surf the Wave

http://goan.com/surflink.html

Log on to this cool site if you want to forecast the biggest waves and find the hottest surfboard stores around.

The World of Sport

http://www.msn.co.uk/sports/

All the latest breaking news and reviews from the world of sport. There's some great competitions too! Whatever your sport, you'll love this site.

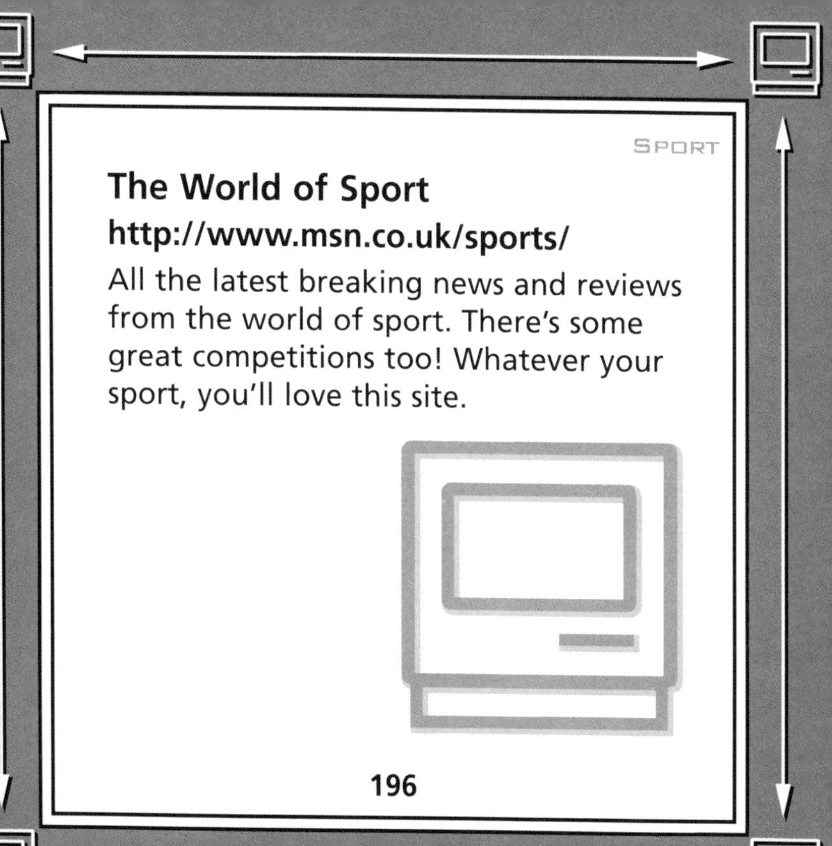

Sporting Life

http://www.sporting-life.com

The famous newspaper is now online and full of news, scores, statistics and betting tips.

Scrum Time

http://www.scrum.com

This was voted one of the best Rugby info sites on the web. Take a look at results, upcoming games and famous quotes.

Eurosport

http://www.eurosport.com

The ever-popular satellite TV channel has gone online, and allows you to check out all that is going on in the world of sport.

Sporting Bet!

http://www.sportingbet.com

This sharp site lets you place a bet on the sport of your choice, and unlike most other betting sites, it's tax-free!

NFL

http://www.nfl.com

This is the official NFL site – catch some of the locker room gossip or just check on the scores.

Ride 'Em Cowboy!

http://www.prorodeo.com

Saddle up and enjoy the Wild West world of rodeo, with the latest on calf-roping, steer-wrestling and bareback riding. Yeehaa!

Watch the Birdie

http://www.golfonline.com

If you're golf crazy, this is just for you! Check out the tournaments, leaderboards, courses and stats right here.

Karate Kid

http://www.karatenet.com

For budding black belts everywhere, a site dedicated to martial arts news and events. Take the online test to see if you could become a martial arts moviestar!

Cricket Unlimited

http://www.cricinfo.org

Find out more about this civilized sport – it's not just about white sweaters and cucumber sandwiches!

Hoop Dreams

http://www.prostar.com/web/northshr/bb-tips.htm

Learn basketball basics at this helpful beginners' site, including offense, defense, dribbling and a huge range of different shots.

Anyone for Tennis?

http://www.tennisone.com

Visit the lesson library, read the worldwide tennis news, and put your questions to the pros at this exciting tennis site.

Turnstep

http://www.turnstep.com

Cyber aerobics are the way of the future – view top aerobic instructors at this motivational site.

Reel Fishing

http://www.where-to-fish.com

Cast your net into the waters – a huge site detailing where you can fish all over the world.

Get Ahead in Tennis

http://www.tennisserver.com

Improve your serve and chat to other enthusiasts at this winning tennis site.

The Davis Cup

http://www.daviscup.org

Relive the past and present Davis Cup action here – it also includes a reference section that details past players and scores.

Ping Pong

http://www.ittf.com

Table Tennis – the game where co-ordination and concentration are the key! Get the latest news and competition info here!

Frisbee Fanatic?

http://www.frisbee.com

Frisbee is gaining respect as a game of skill and cunning, so log on to this hot site to practise throwing and avoiding trees!

Dirtragmag

http://www.dirtragmag.com

'Dirtragmag' is the ezine for all cogheads out there! – if you don't understand the jargon, you'd better get online to read up on it.

Jump!

http://www.aerial.org/

Open the door, hold your breath, and go online for some of the scariest sports known to man. You name it, these guys can organize it for you!

Ski Central

http://www.skicentral.com/

'Skicentral' is the search engine of choice for ski bunnies all over the Net, connecting to over 5,500 snow sites and live snow-cams!

Paddle Power

http://www.paddling.net

Filled with canoeing and kayaking info, this site also offers product reviews, places to paddle, and a boat buyers' guide.

Trial by Pain

http://www.triathletemag.com

If you are mad enough to try it, this is the place to come to get the best in fitness and training regimes.

Cyber Darts

http://www.cyberdarts.com

You may well associate darts with big beer bellies. But this virtual dart site forces you to admit there is actually a lot of skill involved.

Martial Arts Network

http://www.martial-arts-network.com

Before you sign up for a martial arts class, visit this site – it includes lots of details on how to get started.

Sports Halls

http://www.sportshalls.com/search.cfm

Halls of Fame are usually associated with certain sporting arenas, but this one documents sporting legends from around the world.

The Sport of Giants

http://www.nba.com

The official site of the National Basketball Association – check out player profiles and past and present scores.

Rugby Rush

http://www.irfb.com

Comprehensive advice on how to play the game, all the rules, regulations, tournaments, fixtures and results can be found here.

Cricket-Cam

http://www.lords.org/mcc/camview/

Cricket-cam gives you a bird's-eye view of all the latest action at 'Lords'. Mind you, the cam is turned on 24 hours a day even when it is not cricket season!

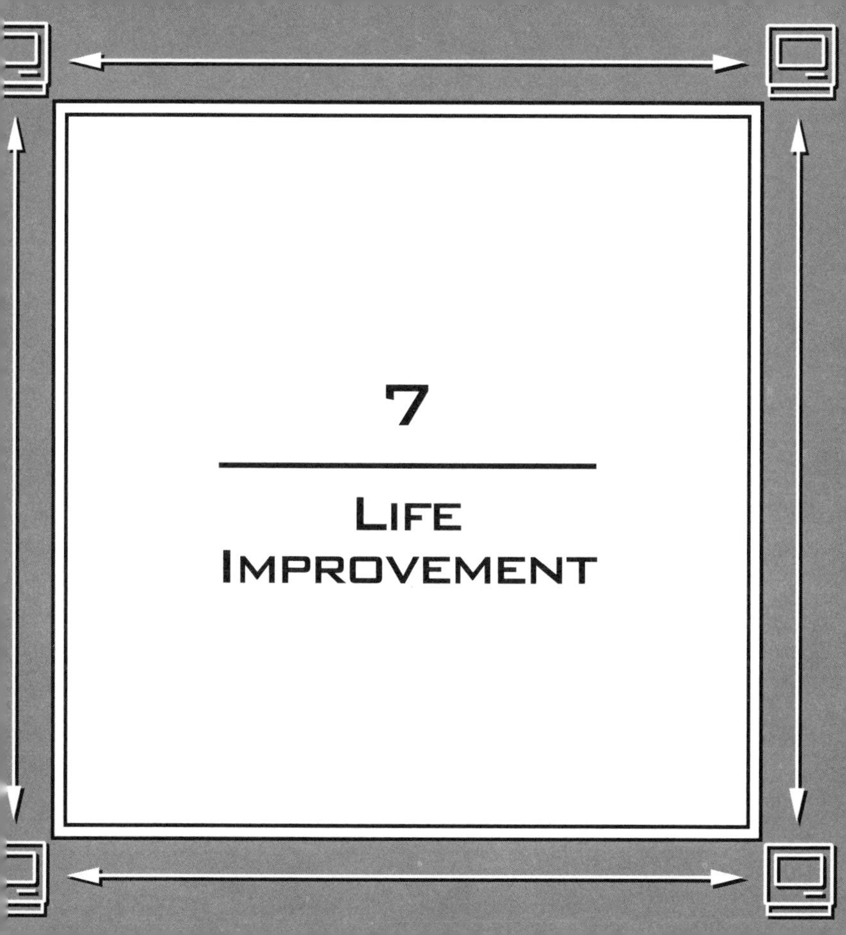

7

Life Improvement

Tips and Products

http://www.beauty.com

For those who haven't got time to go to the beauticians, here is the latest low-down on new products and beauty tips so that you can do it at home!

Beauty Hype

http://www.beautybuzz.com

Throw down that eyelash curler and log onto this site featuring make-up reviews by no-nonsense beauty experts who speak their mind.

Hair Today!

http://www.salonweb.com

What style best suits your face shape and how can you maintain your new hairstyle? The answers are only a mouse-click away!

Emotions

http://www.beme.com

Think about the emotional side of life at this helpful web site that deals with relationships, dating and love.

Heart Warmers

http://www.heartwarmers4u.com

You will either find this site full of inspirational nuggets of positivity or smugly annoying nonsense – but you won't know until you check it out!

Aarrgghh!

http://www.beautynet.com

Are you sick of buying new shampoos each week to try to tame your hair? If so, this virtual helpline will answer this and other beauty queries.

Glamor Puss

http://www.glamour.com

A sharp site revealing fashion 'dos' and 'don'ts' and has a funny section on famous fashion faux pas!

Perfect

http://www.selfgrowth.com

This web site will link you to over 4,000 self-improvement sites – so sip celery juice and get in touch with your inner goodness!

Top to Toe

http://www.healthatoz.com/atoz/default.asp

A one-stop site on complete family health that will answer all your questions and give you tips to keep you fighting fit.

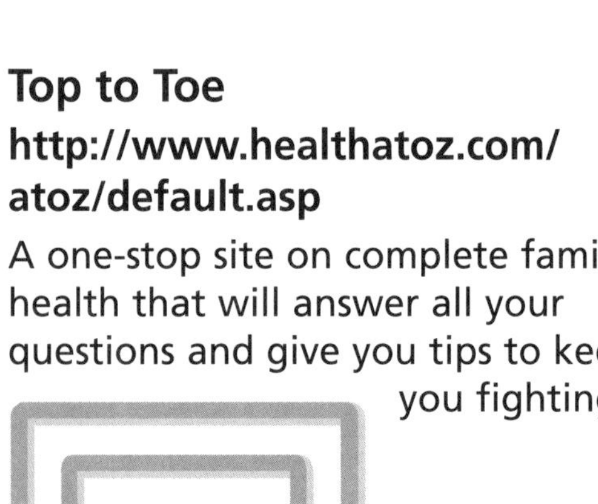

Health and Healing

http://www.hhnews.com

Here are the latest facts on aromatherapy, health, and healing at one motivational and uplifting site.

KidsHealth

http://kidshealth.org/parent

Full of up-to-date info on children's growth, nutrition and fitness, childhood infections, and much more to help give your little ones a good start in life.

Celebrity Copycat!

http://www.hintmag.com

Do you want to look like a star? Well, here you can find hints and all the latest Hollywood gossip!

Natural Health Clinic

http://www.healthy.net/

An easy guide to treating your cold or other illnesses naturally. You may still need a doctor, but it's always good to have an alternative!

Cyberdiet

http://www.cyberdiet.com

Dieting is hard at the best of times – so if you need someone to motivate and help you, click on to this great cyberdiet site.

Slumber Party

http://www.geocities.com/FashionAvenue/catwalk/1159/welcome.html

Put on your pyjamas and join in the activities of the evening, including makeovers, pedicures, manicures and perfect eyebrows!

Homemade Beauty

http://www.allsands.com/Lifestyles/women/homemadebeauty_rrp_gn.html

Save a fortune and use household ingredients to make hair-care, anti-ageing and toning products in the comfort of your own home!

Third Age

http://www.thirdage.com/health/beauty/index.html

Learn how to cut stress, pamper yourself, and boost energy at this site exclusively aimed at those in their Third Age.

Alternative Remedies

http://www.altmedicine.com

This site sorts out all your queries regarding alternative medicine, and if it doesn't have the answer, email Dr Blonz for a speedy reply.

Feeling Sleepy?

http://www.hypnosis.com

Want to improve your love life? Then how about considering hypnosis! Click on to get the low-down.

Virtual Condom

http://www.virtualcondoms.org/

Send a virtual condom to someone you love! Or perhaps somebody who needs reminding!

Hot Tips

http://www.geocities.com/paris/6542/index.html

If you or your partner need a few tips on spicing up your bedroom antics, this fun site will give some good advice.

Shopaholic

http://fb.women.com/fashionandbeauty/

Look out girls! – 24-hour clothes shopping for all tastes and sizes with no crowded changing rooms to annoy you.

Vital Vitamins

http://www.auravita.com

When you're feeling pale and sluggish, a vitamin can often help, so log on here for the lowdown on different types to set you right again.

Dr Koop

http://www.drkoop.com

Consult Dr Koop for informative discussions and medical problem forums, and have a look at the online medical encyclopedia for more health topic info.

Bookstore Bonanza

http://www.uk.bol.com

There's nothing better than a great book, so choose from over 1.5 million at this literary site that features a huge range of subjects.

Suffering in Silence?

http://www.embarrassingproblems.com

From acne to warts, this site deals with health problems that are worrying you and that are difficult to discuss with others.

Virtual Real Estate

http://www.goodmigrations.co.uk/

If it's a UK property you want to shop online for, then you'd better consult this site first as it has everything a home buyer needs including tips and home improvement projects.

Discount Sounds

http://www.cdparadise.com

Buy all the new releases here and read the latest CD reviews.

CD Now

http://www.cdnow.com

Try before you buy at this online music store – listen to bite-sized music tasters and check out the great discounts.

Women's Health

http://www.womens-health.com

Register here for regular tips and advice on women's health, including info on common complaints and their remedies.

E-Music

http://www.emusic.com

This web site allows you to download all your favorite tracks, and if you want to buy the entire CD after that, you can do. Easy!

Global Blooms

http://www.floritel.com

Everyone loves receiving flowers and this global florist delivers to over 190 countries – there's no excuse!

Suited and Booted

http://www.cowtownboots.com

Make a fashion statement with a pair of El Paso rattlesnake cowboy boots. You can order these and a whole host of others at this 'bootiful' site.

Jungle Shopper!

http://www.jungle.com

If the jungle drums are urging you to shop then this is the site for you! With products ranging from computers to films on DVD, there is something to suit everyone!

Go Gadget

http://www.21store.com

Everyone loves a gadget so welcome to the 'Twenty-First Century Store'! They even have glasses to help you see at night!

Fitness Online

http://www.fitnessonline.com

With helpful sections on exercise, nutrition, mind and body, and general health, there's no excuse to veg out in front of the TV tonight!

Kit Bag

http://www.kitbag.com

Maybe fashion isn't your ball game! If you feel more comfortable hanging out in your soccer team's colors, then this web site is for you.

Undie Blues

http://www.kiniki.com

From practical to raunchy, there's lots of underwear to choose from at reasonable prices here.

Personal Shopper

http://www.mysimon.com

If you need expert shopping advice, MySimon will power his way through over 1,000 shops, never stopping until he finds what you're looking for at the lowest possible price. Go Simon!

Search and Shop!

http://botspot.com/search/s-shop.htm

This search agent will take all the hard work out of comparison shopping on a range of items, including CDs, books and products at discounted prices.

Feel the Burn

http://www.workout.com

Sign up with a virtual trainer to create a personalized fitness program especially for you, and you'll soon start to see the results.

Auction Online

http://www.auctionguide.com

Buying goods at an auction can often save you money, and this buzzing site gives you all the tips and info you need to make a successful bid.

Bid Baby!

http://www.ebay.com

Literally hundreds of items up for auction here – bid from anywhere in the world but be aware of shipping and delivery costs!

Fitness Library

http://www.primusweb.com/fitnesspartner/library/libindex.htm

Full of sensible advice on managing your weight, easy nutrition, and getting and staying active, this is one library where you won't be fined for late returns!

Feng Shui

http://www.worldoffengshui.com/

Find the latest tips on one of the first fully comprehensive Feng Shui sites and check out what has been done to the 'White House'!

Real Self-help

http://www.psychwww.com/resource/selfhelp.htm

Exceptionally helpful site for those who need some advice and support on everyday anxieties from others who have suffered similar problems themselves.

Uri Online

http://www.uri-geller.com/

Find out if you have the gift of psychic insight from the man who has made a living out of forks and spoons. Yes, it's Uri Geller and his site of wonders!

Stonehenge

http://www.activemind.com/Mysterious/Topics/Stonehenge

The mystical home of the ancient druid site near Salisbury in England. Check out the fascinating theories about how the huge stone 'temple' came to be.

Meditation Network

http://www.thoughtaday.com

A good site for those who want to improve their powers of concentration – log on for a meditative thought for the day!

Fashion Net

http://www.fashion.net

Who's hot, who's not, who's wearing what, where to get it, and who designed it? All your fashion questions are answered here.

The Emporium

http://www.fengshuiemporium.com/

This is the place to shop for all your Feng Shui requirements – did you know that if you leave your toilet seat up, you'll lose all your money?

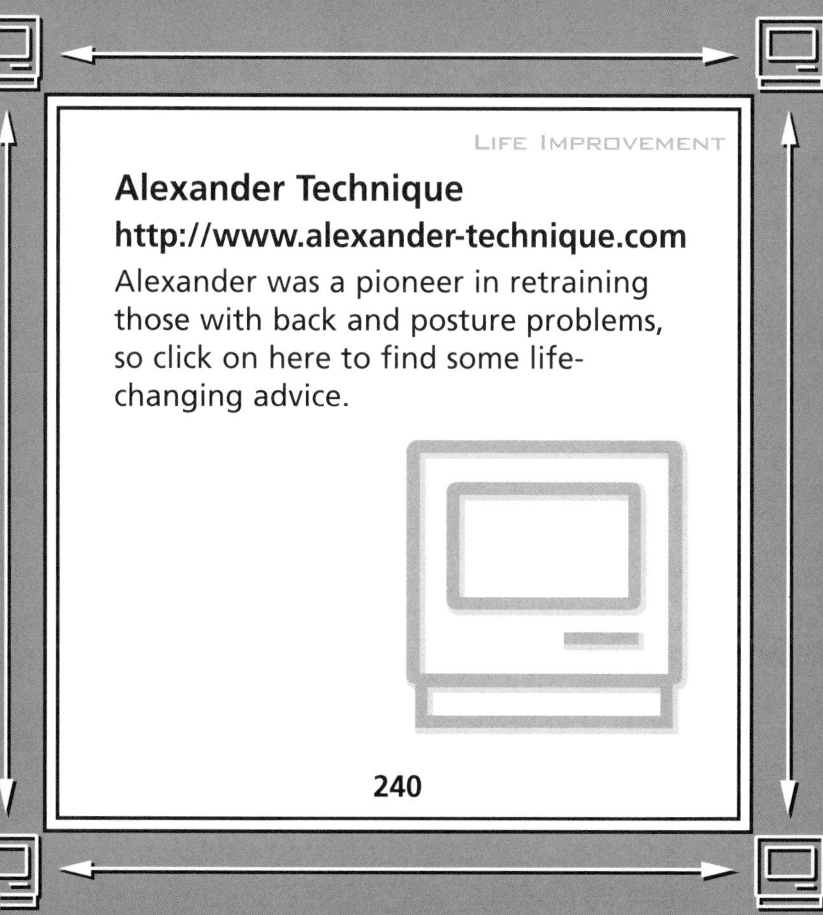

Alexander Technique

http://www.alexander-technique.com

Alexander was a pioneer in retraining those with back and posture problems, so click on here to find some life-changing advice.

Fashion Guide

http://www.fashionguide.com

Throw out those pixie boots and leg warmers and get the latest trends, fashion news, and beauty tips at this in-depth fashion site.

Oops!

http://www.remindu.net

Too busy to remember birthdays and anniversaries? No excuses now with this invaluable web site that will remind you of important dates!

Don't Shop, Swap!

http://www.webswappers.com

Register your goodies at this site and ask what you want for it! Everything from games to antiques are swapped here!

Beauty and Soul

http://www.beautysoul.com

Updated daily, this health and beauty site includes the season's fashions and a beauty basics section to get you started on your way to the 'Miss World' competition!

Drug Store

http://www.drugstore.com

Buy all your medical, beauty and pharmaceutical products at this one-stop online pharmacy.

Set Up On Your Own

http://smallbusiness.yahoo.com

Everything you need to know about setting up your own business, from office supplies through to taxes, at this easy-to-follow site.

Dating Know-how

http://www.wildxangel.com

Dating has gone online, so log on to this site to find out the rules and 'dos' and 'don'ts' of love on the web.

Life Goes On

http://www.divorcesupport.com

Sometimes you have to say 'Goodbye' in order to move forward – visit this divorce web site full of helpful and informative material.

Love Heart

http://www.justmove.org

Heart disease is a major killer and the only way to avoid it is to get healthy – here you will find incentives and info to get you moving!

Model Behavior

http://www.models.com

Do you have what it takes? Read articles here on how to become a model and how to build a personal portfolio to help you become the next Cindy Crawford.

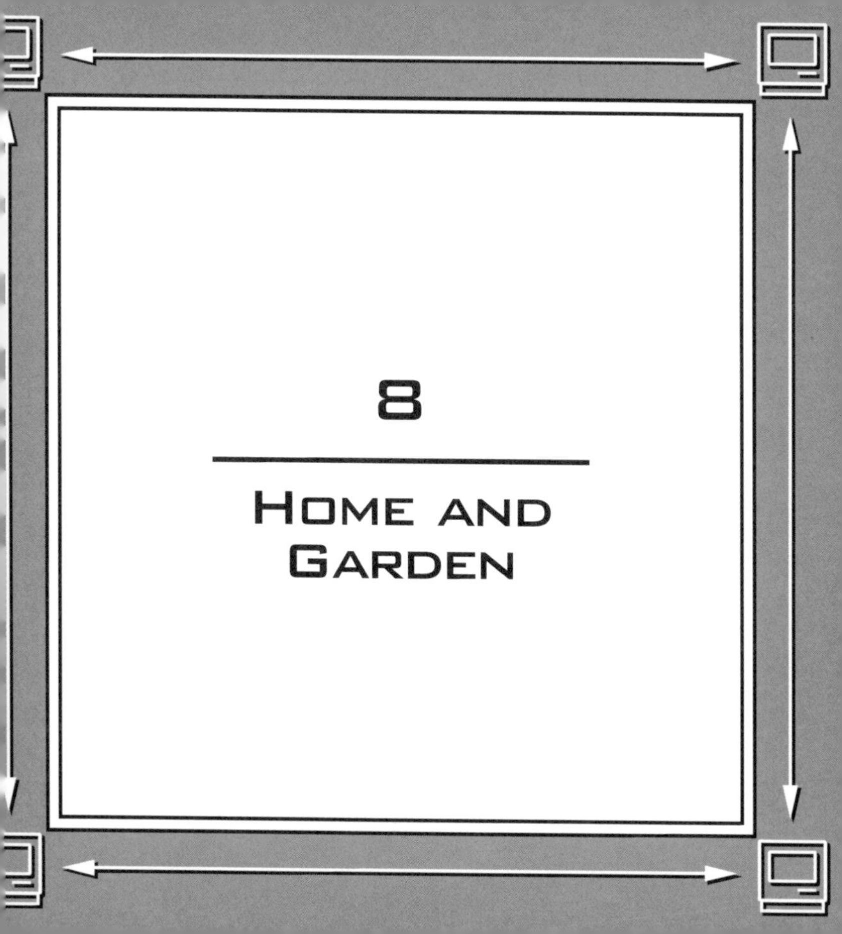

8

Home and Garden

House and Home

http://www.bhg.com/bhg/househome/index.jhtm

Crammed full of tips on everything from making a coffee table to landscape lighting. Your home will be ship shape in no time.

National Gardening

http://www.garden.org

This site includes a gardening tip of the day, an online dictionary of gardening terms, and even e-cards that you can send to other gardening fanatics.

Online Encyclopedia

http://www.bhg.com/

This bumper site specializes in advice on fix and repair, plant guides and moving house – thrash your ideas around with other enthusiasts.

Neighbors from Hell

http://www.hud.gov/complaints/decpcontract.cfm

What can you do when you're living next door to the Addams family? This smart site reveals your rights regarding neighbors, landlords and contractors.

Home Tips

http://www.resourcehelp.com/welcome.htm

Before you pick up that power tool, check this useful search engine that has tons of links to useful home and garden sites.

Furniture Wizard

http://www.furniturewizard.com

Has that coffee stain removed the veneer finish on your table? Don't panic! – 'Furniture Wizard' can fix it and other things too.

Take It Apart

http://www.hometips.com

For the very handy person, a step-by-step guide to tearing your house apart and making it look worth a million dollars!

Home Arts

http://www.homearts.com

This US-based site will do everything but step through the door and hand you a paintbrush – it even helps you choose which fabric is suitable!

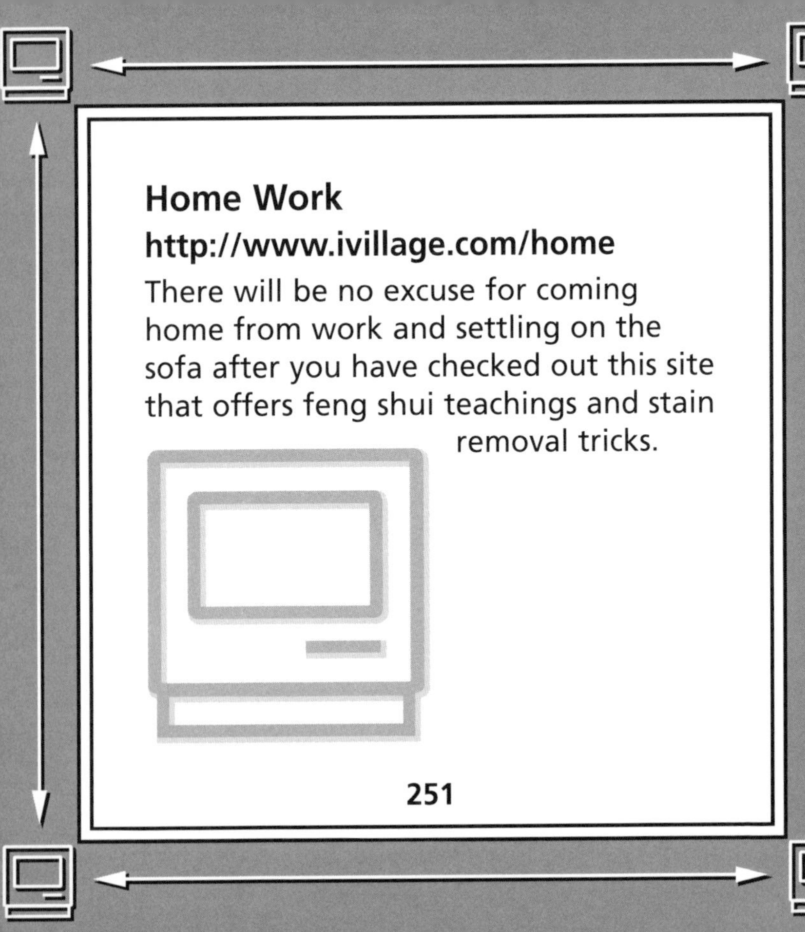

Home Work

http://www.ivillage.com/home

There will be no excuse for coming home from work and settling on the sofa after you have checked out this site that offers feng shui teachings and stain removal tricks.

Green Fingers

http://www.dailypress.com/features/home/garden

Share gardening tips and read helpful articles on lawn care, the best tools, caring for trees and shrubs, and much much more.

Creative with Concrete

http://www.oldcastle.com/home.html

Enhance an already beautiful landscape by adding to it! This web site specializes in concrete landscaping products to make the most of your garden.

Tim the Tool Man

http://www.geocities.com/hollywood/set/7798/index.html

Fans of the hit sitcom 'Home Improvement', listen up! Relive the highlights here and see what Tim and the family are up to now!

More Power!

http://www.tcmn.com/hsn/home.html

Get online now for a free newsletter that is vital for those about to embark on a home improvement project.

Martha Stewart Rules

http://www.marthastewart.com

Homemaker guru, Martha Stewart's one-stop site is filled with easy decorating ideas and tips and advice on collecting, lighting, cooking and gardening.

Natural Handyman

http://www.naturalhandyman.com

No, this doesn't mean home improvement in the nude! This superb site will get professionals and beginners alike in touch with their inner power drill!

Start 'Em Early

http://www.geocities.com/EnchantedForest/Glade/3313

A gardening site for kids of all ages, where you can find out all about kid-friendly plants and other plant facts.

Interior Heaven

http://interiordec.about.com

Keep up with the latest interior decorating trends and learn new DIY techniques at this varied home decorating site that will make you the envy of your neighbors.

In the Workshop

http://www.intheworkshop.com/indexframe.htm

Fancy a bit of furniture making but don't know where to start? Here is a step-by-step guide to building everything from a barbecue caddie to wooden toys.

Décor Delights

http://www.decordelights.com/decordel.html

Learn the art of decorative painting at this fun site that provides step-by-step lessons for both beginners and kids, and also tips and advice.

Fine Gardening

http://www.taunton.com/fg/index.htm

Excellent landscape ezine filled with practical gardening tips and advice, as well as stories written by gardeners in the know.

Green Fingers

http://www.planters2.com

'Planters2' are minerals that help your organic vegetables flourish – they are safe, have met organic standards for over 50 years, and are at this site!

Virtual Store

http://www.delvalmall.com/virtualdelco/homegarden.html

For all your landscaping and gardening supplies, this virtual store offers discounted prices and a secure-ordering process.

Read First!

http://www.bookbuyer.com/

Before you knock down that supporting wall, check out this site containing 4,000 discounted books on home improvement topics.

Living Home

http://www.livinghome.com

Affordable and imaginative ideas on how to achieve that high-tech kitchen, or a complete remodel of your bathroom.

Restoration

http://ne.essortment.com/howtorestoref_rudk.htm

Do you have desks, tables and chairs that need a new lease of life? It's fun, easy and inexpensive and this site will show you how.

Planet Improvement

http://www.shopperscatalog.com/

A huge online store that stocks over 30,000 products in hardware, electrical goods and lighting – home improvement heaven!

Kids Can Sew!

http://ok.essortment.com/kidcansew_rzcq.htm

Can't be bothered to stitch those new curtains yourself? Then get the kids to do it! This site will show them how to get started.

Home Sweet Home

http://www.homeideas.com

Order past and present issues of popular '*Today's Homeowner*' magazine here to solve those niggling house problems.

Modern Gardener

http://www.alternativegarden.com

This amazing site is for the seriously modern gardener – achieve the outdoor space of your dreams here!

Home Made Décor

http://www.homemadesimple.com/easydecor/index.shtml

Do you know a credenza from a cornice? Well, here is a site that promises interior design made simple and offers a large database of projects for you to try.

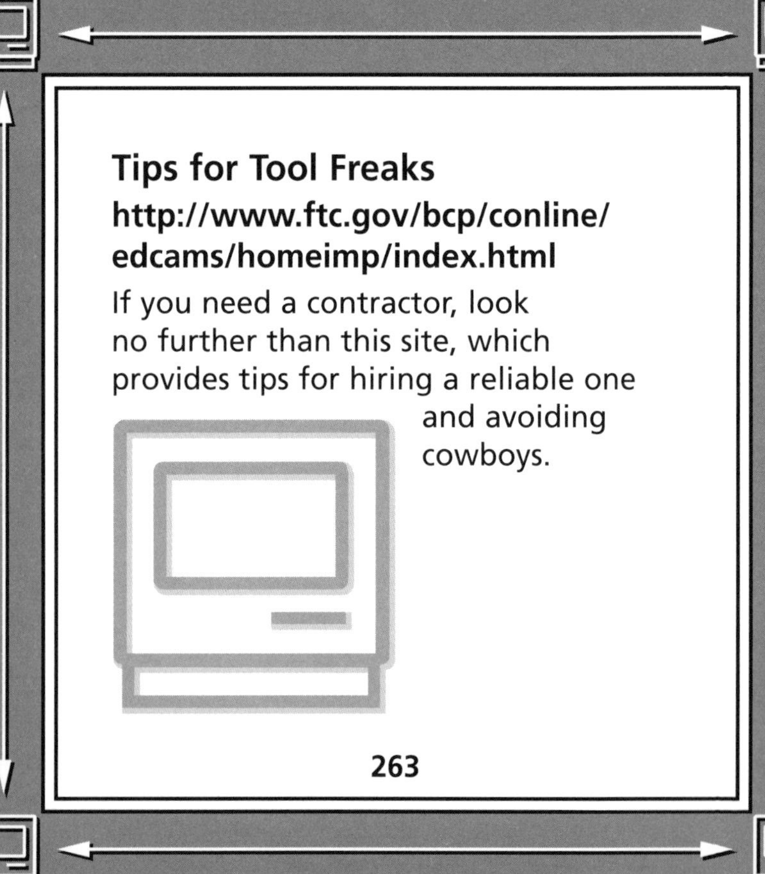

Tips for Tool Freaks

http://www.ftc.gov/bcp/conline/edcams/homeimp/index.html

If you need a contractor, look no further than this site, which provides tips for hiring a reliable one and avoiding cowboys.

Hip Hop Hydroponics

http://www.gtghydroponics.com/

You can order your much-needed hydroponics supplies over the Net, as 'GTG Hydroponics' have a huge range of indoor and outdoor gardening supplies.

Happy Stitching

http://www.coatsfabra.es/en/1/how.html

Create beautiful homemade furnishings by following the 'How To' techniques in embroidery, crochet, sewing and knitting shown here.

Hortus

http://www.hortus.com

This online magazine solves problems and gives advice to 'intelligent and lively-minded gardeners'. Log on to see if they think you're one!

Garden Guides

http://www.gardenguides.com

Containing hundreds of interesting articles and a wealth of gardening info, this green site also has a helpful flower, veg, and herb guide.

Weekend Gardener

http://www.chestnut-sw.com/diction.htm

A range of gardening dictionaries and glossaries can be found here, including gardening terms, botanical terms and pesticide guides.

Gnome World

http://www.fulcrum-gardening.com

If you have a family of gnomes in your garden, then the green bug has bitten you and you'll want all the gardening books available here!

Global Diggers

http://www.gardenweb.com

Exchange ideas with gardeners from all over the globe – it helps lighten the load by sharing with fellow diggers!

Internet Alert!

http://www.learning.lib.vt.edu/garden.html

A friendly site that looks at the effect the Internet will have on the future of gardening – if you are wracked with insomnia over this, log on to find the answer.

Shrubs Direct

http://www.shrubsdirect.com

Order something colorful, be it a rose or a tulip, direct from Cheshire in England, and browse among 900 flowering beauties to add that something extra to your garden.

Pond Plan

http://www.gardeningbc.com

This is a particularly helpful site to check if you are planning to build a pond or landscape your back yard.

Organic Harmony

http://www.organicgardening.com

Organic gardening is the purest way to grow your fresh fruit and vegetables, and this site is one of the best sources of info about growing an organic garden.

Water Keeper

http://www.watergardening.com/

If you are a pond keeper and feel isolated because your neighbors have flower gardens, click on this online magazine to catch up on pond news and gossip.

City Slicker

http://www.nygardener.com

Written originally for New Yorkers, the plan at this site can be adapted by all city dwellers keen to make a natural garden out of a concrete jungle.

Tropicano

http://www.tropicalgardening.com

Ever dreamt of a tropical garden to hang your hammock in? Make it a reality by checking out the info on tropical plants at this site.

Virtual Gardener

http://www.gardenmag.com

A gardening ezine with organic roots that is bursting with plant profiles, tips and tales, and even a virtual store for you to visit.

Gateway to Gardening

http://www.gardennet.com

Are you a total beginner? If you are liable to plant bulbs upside down, log on and learn!

Green World

http://www.gardenersworld.beeb.com

A great starting point for anyone wishing to revamp their garden, and all the info comes from the great British television institution that is the BBC.

Garden Tutorials

http://www.etera.com/school/TutorialCreator/view/tutorialdefaultID=25018.asp?sp=11&Src

Info on indoor and outdoor gardening here. You can learn everything from building a dry stone wall to drying flowers in a microwave!

Family Gardening

http://www.familygardening.com

Here you will find tips on making gardening fun for the whole family – where there's earth, there's a way!

Vegetable Gardening Handbook

http://edis.ifas.ufl.edu/MENU_VH:VH

A comprehensive site featuring gardening advice on growing veggies and their uses, it also features helpful info on irrigation and pest control.

Fantasy Foliage

http://www.fantasy-gardening.com

This web site revolves around a fantasy guessing game – the slightly deranged premise being to predict how long it will take for a particular plant to grow!

Garden Line Online

http://www.jerrybaker.com

Gardening guru, Jerry Baker's site is filled with household and gardening tips that promise to pep up your plants and freshen up your flowers.

Suss Out the Seasons!

http://www.chestnut-sw.com/

Updated weekly with vital information on when and how you should plant seeds, this site means you don't have to worry about seasonal changes!

Poetry Time

http://www.gardendigest.com/index.htm

Gardens can evoke feelings of joy and love, which is why this web site aims to make you run outside and hug your daffodils.

Garden Helper

http://www.thegardenhelper.com

If you have never tested your green thumbs before, this site will help novices and beginners experience the joys of gardening for the first time.

Gardening at Home

http://www.geocities.com/RainForest/5741

A straightforward, no nonsense site that features plant-care advice, as well as a stunning garden tour to inspire you.

A Life Garden

http://www.alifegarden.com

For all nasty-minded gardeners out there, here's your chance to get back at those annoying mosquitoes. Check it out!

Home Store

http://www.homstore.com/ Home_Improvement/default.asp

Containing a huge searchable database of topics, this site also offers advice on homeowner survival kits, energy saving tips and decorating advice.

Piece of Paradise!

http://www.bytheinch.com/buy.htm

For a measly $19.99 you can become the proud owner of a square inch of heaven with a deed to prove it!

Virtual Gardener

http://www.gardenmag.com

An online magazine that will help both the amateur and professional gardener alike. If you have any queries, stick it on the online notice board and you'll soon have an answer!

LAGOON WEB SITE

Games, Books, Puzzles and Gizmos

Visit the Lagoon Web Site to view a staggering range of fantastic games, puzzles and books to suit all.

www.lagoongames.com

OTHER TITLES BY LAGOON BOOKS

Brain-Boosting Puzzle Books

Brain-Boosting Quantum Puzzles
(1-902813-52-9)

Brain-Boosting Cryptology Puzzles
(1-902813-54-5)

Brain-Boosting Sequence Puzzles
(1-902813-53-7)

Brain-Boosting Cryptic Puzzles
(1-902813-21-9)

Brain-Boosting Visual Logic Puzzles
(1-902813-20-0)

Brain-Boosting Lateral Thinking Puzzles
(1-902813-22-7)

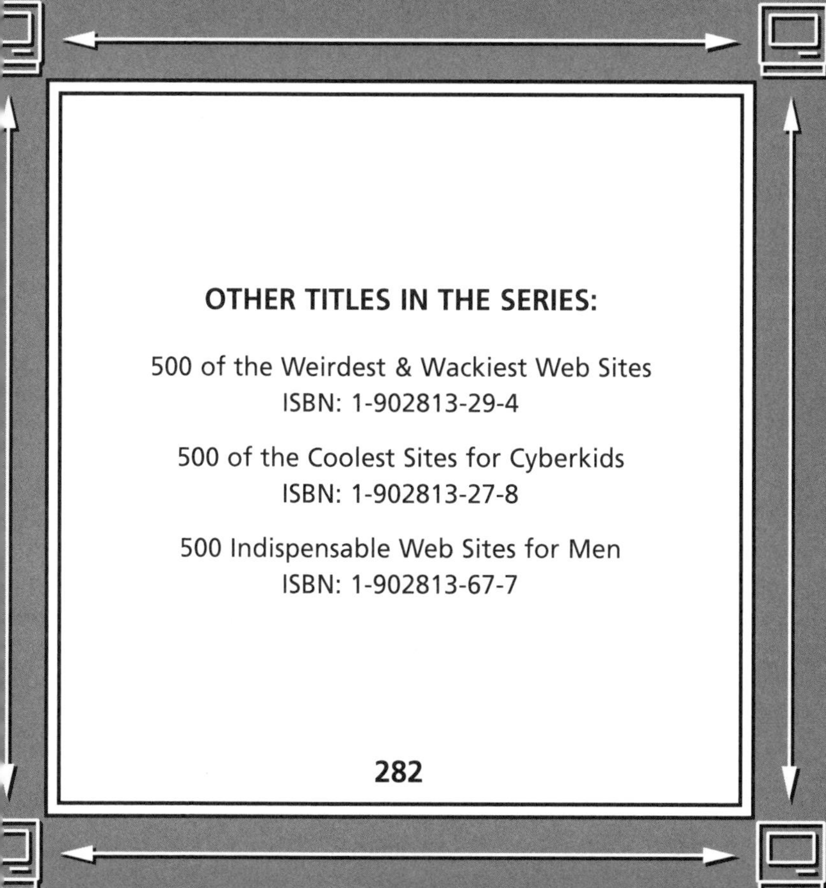

OTHER TITLES IN THE SERIES:

500 of the Weirdest & Wackiest Web Sites
ISBN: 1-902813-29-4

500 of the Coolest Sites for Cyberkids
ISBN: 1-902813-27-8

500 Indispensable Web Sites for Men
ISBN: 1-902813-67-7

LAGOON
BOOKS